Reconstructing Devotion

Rediscovering Indian Literary Classics

(ISSN - 0972-0111)

1. *Taittirīya Upaniṣad*: With the Original Text in Sanskrit and Roman transliteration. Translation with an Exhaustive Commentary; by Muni Narayana Prasad. (ISBN 978-81-246-0014-6)

2, 4-5. *Bṛhadāraṇyaka Upaniṣad*: With Original Text in Roman transliteration. English Translation and Appendices; by Nitya Chaitanya Yati; Vol. 1: Madhu Kāṇḍa; Vol. 2: Muni Kāṇḍa; Vol. 3: Khila Kāṇḍa. (ISBN 978-81-246-0008-5)

3. *Kena Upaniṣad*: With the Original Text in Sanskrit and Roman transliteration. Translation with an Extensive Commentary; by Muni Narayana Prasad. (ISBN 978-81-246-0034-4)

6. *Muṇḍaka Upaniṣad*: With the Original Text in Sanskrit and Roman transliteration. Translation with an Exhaustive Commentary; by Muni Narayana Prasad. (ISBN 978-81-246-0105-1)

7. *Kaṭha Upaniṣad*: With the Original Text in Sanskrit and Roman transliteration. Translation with an Exhaustive Commentary; by Muni Narayana Prasad. (ISBN 978-81-246-0110-5)

8. *Praśna Upaniṣad*: With the Original Text in Sanskrit and Roman transliteration. Translation with an Extensive Commentary; by Muni Narayana Prasad. (ISBN 978-81-246-0129-5)

9. *Aitareya Upaniṣad*: With the Original Text in Sanskrit and Roman transliteration. Translation with an Extensive Commentary; by Muni Narayana Prasad. (ISBN 978-81-246-0142-6)

10. *Śrī Dakṣiṇāmūrti Stotram* of *Śrī Śaṅkarācārya*; with the commentary *Tattvaprakāśikā*; by Swami Tattvavidananda Saraswati; Edited by Puppala B. (ISBN 978-81-246-0210-2)

11. *Āditya Hṛdayam*: With the Commentary *Tattvaprakāśikā*; by Swami Tattvavidananda Saraswati (ISBN 978-81-246-0231-7)

12. *Vāstuśāstra*: Ancient Indian Architecture and Civil Engineering — Retrospects and Prospects; by Rahul Kumar Altekar (ISBN 978-81-246-0246-1)

13. *Gaṇapati Upaniṣad*: With the Commentary *Tattvaprakāśikā*; by Swami Tattvavidananda Saraswati (ISBN 978-81-246-0265-2)

14. *Life's Pilgrimage Through the Gītā*; by Swami Muni Narayana Prasad (ISBN 978-81-246-0310-9)

15. *Chāndogya Upaniṣad*; by Swami Muni Narayana Prasad (ISBN 978-81-246-0374-1)

16. *Īśavāsya and Māṇḍūkya Upaniṣad*; by Swami Muni Narayana Prasad (ISBN 978-81-246-0492-2)

Redicovering Indian Literary Classics, no. 17

Reconstructing Devotion

Through Nārada Bhakti Sūtra

Alka Tyagi

DK
PRINTWORLD
Publishers of Indian Traditions

Cataloging in Publication Data — DK
[Courtesy: D.K. Agencies (P) Ltd. <docinfo@dkagencies.com>]

Tyagi, Alka, author.
Reconstructing devotion through Nārada bhakti sūtra / Alka Tyagi.
pages cm – (Redicovering Indian literary classics ; no. 17).
English and Sanskrit (Sanskrit in Devanagari and roman).
Includes bibliographical references.

1. Nāradasūtra – Criticism, interpretation, etc. 2. Bhakti. 3. God (Hinduism) – Worship and love. I. Nāradasūtra. II. Nāradasūtra. English. III. Title. IV. Series: Redicovering Indian literary classics ; no. 17.

LCC BL1214.32.B53T93 2018 | DDC 294.54 23

ISBN: 978-81-246-0954-5
First published in India in 2019

Printed and published by:
D.K. Printworld (P) Ltd.
Regd. Office: Vedaśrī, F-395, Sudarshan Park
(Metro Station: E.S.I. Hospital), New Delhi - 110015
Phones: (011) 2545 3975, 2546 6019
e-mail: indology@dkprintworld.com
Website: www.dkprintworld.com

Dedicated to the gurus

Swami Niranjanananda Saraswati

and

Swami Satyasangananda Saraswati

who personify Supreme Love

अवधूता युगन युगन हम योगी
आवै न जाये मिटें न कबहुँ
सबद अनाहत भोगी
सब ठौर पर जमात हमरी
सब ठौर पर मेला
हम सब माय सब हैं हम माय
हम हैं बहुरि अकेला
हम हैं सिद्ध समाधि हम ही
हम मौनी हम बोले
रूप सरूप अरूप दिखाके
हम माहीं हम तो खेलें
कहे कबीर सुनो भाई साधो
रही नहीं कोई इच्छा
अपनी मढी में आप मैं डोलूं
खेलूं सहज स्वेच्छा

— कबीर

Avadhūta, for eons I am *yogī*
Not born, I don't die
I am enjoyer of soundless sound
At all place I have community
At all places there is festival
I am in everyone, everyone in me
I am alone amidst many
I am the *siddha*, I am the *samādhi*
I am silent, I am the one who speaks
Showing myself in form and in formless
I play with myself
Listen Oh *sādho*! Kabīr says
There is no desire in me
I swing joyfully in my dwelling
Play by my own free will.

— Kabīr

Preface

TOWARDS the end of 1990s, I began to visit Sivananda Ashram of Divine Life Society at Rishikesh. I often got a chance to interact with resident *sṁnyāsin*s there on teachings of Swami Sivananda Saraswati. During one such visit, I met Swami Devbhaktananda, who used to work at the printing press of the Ashram. He followed the footsteps of his *guru* Swami Sivananda and used to distribute many Ashram publication texts free of cost. I was also fortunate to receive the *Nārada Bhakti Sūtra* along with many more books of Swami Sivananda Saraswati as *prasāda* from him.

This slim, small, copy of the *Nārada Bhakti Sūtra* with coffee-coloured cover page was translated by Swami Sivananda Saraswati himself. For me, all the books of Swamiji carry his vibrations. I feel as if his compassion still flows through his writings. His words are alive with energy even though he left his mortal body long ago. The *Nārada Bhakti Sūtra* began to speak to me through Swami Sivanandaji's little booklet.

Coincidentally, I had begun to revive my Sanskrit studies and was keen on reading texts in simple Sanskrit. In this regard also, the *Nārada Bhakti Sūtra* served my purpose as it is one of the easiest texts for a Sanskrit language learner from linguistic point of view. I was happy to read it as I could understand the *sūtra*s without looking at the English translation given below.

The second *sūtra – sa tvasmin paramapreamsvarūpa* (*Bhakti* is of the form of supreme love) – connected me to the whole text in a deeper way. I began to understand that *bhakti* is not merely worshipping the image of God in a temple, or fasting or conducting rituals. *Bhakti* is all about expanding the boundaries of loving space in our life.

In our routine existence, we consider love to be something that we shower over those who are related to us by blood relations, friendship, marriage, attachment, etc. Nārada shows us that *bhakti* is a capacity to love everyone and everything in the creation without any human-made restrictions of caste, class, gender, species, genus and so on and so forth.

At first glance, the *Nārada Bhakti Sūtra* appears to be didactic and religious in spirit but another look at it reveals many more facets of the text that relate to personal experience of that supreme love by which the *bhakti* is defined. There are two streams of thought that go hand in hand in the text. First line of thought indicates *bhakti*, the Supreme Love as a progressive path towards a goal. The second line of thought conveys *bhakti* as a path which is simultaneously the goal as well. I understand that for those of us who are clearly emotionally inclined, it is easy to choose the second line of thought where *bhakti* is the goal in itself. Such people should just tune in to the love that flows from their heart and should just channel it in an egalitarian manner to all.

However, those of us who are intellectually inclined will find it very difficult to exercise unconditional love. For them, the first line of thought will work better. They can consciously choose *bhakti*, the path of love as a progressive path towards fulfilment and joy in life. For them, the rules of truth, non-violence, non-duality along with the rituals of *ekādaśdhā-bhakti* (the elevenfold *bhakti*) as prescribed by Sage Narada could be helpful techniques. These rules and rituals are nothing but practices to rouse the emotional energy present in every human being in its fullness and to direct it in a positive direction.

We get a glimpse of the nature of joy of full love in the description of *ekāntin bhakta*s or those who are completely soaked in love in the *sūtra* 68 of the text. When such people meet others of their kind, it is like Rāma meeting Bharata during his *vanavāsa* or like Ramakrishna Paramahansa meeting Narendranatha, the future Swami Vivekananda, the first time.

With a wish that love prevails on the planet and the forces of hatred and violence are sublimated by dominance of egalitarian love, I humbly offer this translation to the seekers of Absolute Love.

Alka Tyagi

26 November 2018

New Delhi

Contents

Acknowledgements

I WOULD like to thank Swami Devabhaktananda Saraswati of Sivananda Ashram, Rishikesh who teaches *Nārada-Bhaktisūtra* at the Vedanta Forest Akademi of Divine Life Society, Rishikesh. Before his role as a teacher, he was serving at the Printing Press of the Ashram and there he first introduced the text to me by offering a copy of the Swami Sivananda's pithy translation of *Nārada-Bhaktisūtra* many years ago. I would also like to thank Swami Padmanabhananda Saraswati, the secretary of Divine Life Society, who never denied my request to reside at the Sivananda Ashram and thus gave me ample number of opportunities to partake of the devotional environment of the whole place.

I would like to thank Mr. Bernd Fellner, who offered to become the first reader of my manuscript. His suggestions have been very helpful in putting the introductory part of text together.

I would also like to acknowledge cooperation of my publisher, Shri Susheel Kumar Mittal ji, in helping me to prepare this text for publication at many levels. I am grateful for his compassion and for the way he motivates me with his positive words.

2 July 2018 **Alka Tyagi**
Berlin

Introduction

Bhakti: The Loving Devotion

BHAKTI (loving devotion) is an intense inclination to relate with the unseen and the intangible in the universe. It is a rendezvous with all-embracing living energy. *Bhakti* creates a link with the inner self on one hand and with the supreme mystical force on the other. For a believer, devotion serves as a psychological aid to unfold and realize the full potential in life and to cross over the conflict situations in a non-belligerent manner. It has its origin in human race's desire and capacity for love.

Devotion as deep love for the Highest has been wrapped in religious accoutrements thereby making it incomprehensible to the atheist and the agnostic. I have chosen to reread the *Nārada Bhakti Sūtra* in the modern scenario in which it appears to be very naive and old-fashioned to imagine a god sitting in heaven and looking benignly at each one of us. Perhaps, it is rather easy to believe in a cosmic principle which has Supreme Power and therefore could be omnipotent, omnipresent and omniscient. The *Nārada Bhakti Sūtra* is a very basic religious text on *bhakti*, the loving devotion. This text has its relevance in present situation because it suggests exceedingly simple techniques to develop and mediate human emotional energy in the direction where it can experience the Supreme Principle (described as God in this text).

Classical Form of Bhakti

Classical *bhakti,* as an act of devotion and worship of God, is an expression of individual bond with the Supreme Reality. Classical *bhakti* emerged in a religious context and is embedded in a discursive field imbued with religious and mythological trappings. However, *bhakti* can also mean a way of being. *Bhakti* is erroneously perceived as a religion-specific act or path due to the religious paraphernalia associated with it. Hence it is frowned upon and rejected as a superstition by those who do not believe in any specific religion. Nevertheless, for a theist, *bhakti* serves as a necessary anchor that helps one to sail smoothly through his/her life.

In Hinduism, *bhakti* has gradually evolved into a complete philosophical system over the centuries. In the Vedas, the idea of *bhakti* as devotion is not so well pronounced. The Vedic priest repeatedly asks the question, कस्मै देवाय हविषा विधेम? – *kasmai devāya haviṣā vidhema*? (To which god, shall we offer our oblations?). Among the Upaniṣads, the *Śvetāśvatara Upaniṣad* is the first to mention *bhakti*:

> यस्य देवे परा भक्तिर्यथा देवे तथा गुरौ । तस्यैते कथिता ह्यर्थः प्रकाशन्ते महात्मनः प्रकाशन्ते महात्मन इति ॥
>
> *yasya deve parā bhaktiryathā deve tathā gurau* । *tasyaite kathitā hyarthāḥ prakāśante mahātmanaḥ prakāśante mahātmana iti* ॥
>
> – 6.23
>
> Those who have supreme devotion in God and the same devotion in *guru*, the supreme truths illuminate through these great souls.

It is in the epics and Purāṇas that *bhakti* appears as a subject of discussion as well as experience. Lakṣmaṇa, Bharata, Śabarī and Hanumān come across as great devotees of Śrī Rāma in the *Rāmāyaṇa* however *bhakti* is systematically exposited as *bhakti-yoga* in the *Bhagavadgītā*. The Purāṇas are the best documents of *bhakti* as they depict legends of gods and deities narrated from the devotional perspective. *Bhakti* finds its best expression in the *Bhāgavata Purāṇa*. This Purāṇa describes *gopikās'* legendary Kṛṣṇa *bhakti*. Their devotional love for Kṛṣṇa explains various mystical dimensions of existence.

Idea of a Personal God in Classical Bhakti

Conception of cosmic order in Hinduism consists of creation, maintenance and withdrawal. After creation there is need to maintain and then to withdraw it as well so that the creation can run its full course. Evil and good coexist as two dimensions of this order and must be in some kind of balance for a sustainable existence. Sometimes however the evil gets an upper hand and threatens the existence of all good. When the virtues of all good human beings joined together are not able to uphold the harmony, then the Supreme Power (omniscient, omnipotent, omnipresent) takes *avatāra* in human form. As a form of God, this *avatāra* retains its special powers and pushes the evil back into its place. It is the effulgence and excellence of His life on earth in human form that makes the *avatāra* most adorable. Since He is a descent of, omniscient, omnipotent and omnipresent Supreme, He is loved even when His bodily form has passed away. This is the idea behind the Hindu pantheon of gods who take different forms. The *bhakta* (devotee) can choose from a range of God's *avatāra*s in Hindu pantheon. An *avatāra* invokes love in a devotee due to the auspiciousness, effulgence, beauty, virtues and the heroic legends associated with Him. Devotees take to a form of God which is most appealing to them – Rāma, Kṛṣṇa, Śiva, Kālī, Durgā, Lakṣmī, Sarasvatī, Gaṇeśa, Ṣaṇmukha and so on.

The form of the deity that a *bhakta* chooses as focus of his/

her devotion, is known as *iṣṭa*, the chosen personal form of God. The devotee fixes his/her devotion on a personal god due to deep faith in the existence of God. The faith in God is a prerequisite on the path of classical *bhakti*.

Classical *bhakti* also includes rituals which are derived from everyday acts in routine human existence. Everyday human acts are sanctified with rituals, and rites are offered symbolically to the chosen deity. Best example of such a ritual is the *ṣoḍaśopcāra-pūjā*, the most popular form of worship offered to a deity. It employs sixteen acts of offering loving devotion to the deity. The *bhakta* treats the deity like a personification of excellence, a very respectable and lovable being and offers everything that should be offered as a loving gesture to an adorable person with extraordinary virtues. First eight acts relate to fulfilling the needs of the body – welcome of the deity (*āhvāna*), offering a seat (*āsana*), washing the feet (*pādya*), offering water for cleaning hands (*arghya*) and mouth (*ācamana*), bathing the deity (*snānam*), offering the clothes and jewels (*vastra*) and changing the sacred thread (*janeū/yajñopavīta*). The next eight acts relate to fulfilling the requirements of the senses – offering aroma (*gandha*), offering flower (*puṣpa*), burning incense (*dhūpa*), waving of light (*dīpaka*), offering food (*naivedyam*), offering beetle nut (*tāmbūlam*) and finally offering respect with joined hands (*puṣpāñjali*). This kind of *bhakti* presupposes a temple or a sanctum sanctorum. Although it is exoteric in nature, it allows the devotee to practise it as mental worship (*manas-pūjā*) at the esoteric level. Just as the mind is considered to be superior to the body and the senses, in the same way the mental and emotional worship is considered to be superior to the external worship which is considered as grosser in comparison. Tantra and *bhakti* scriptures often emphasize on the involvement and engagement of the complete self –

body, senses, mind and emotions – in the act of devotion.

Bhakti in Ancient Times

In north India, the Vedic wisdom conceived the supreme power of the universe in the form of awe-inspiring forces of nature – rain, thunder, the sun, the moon, water, air and so on. In the Upaniṣadic period, first mention of word *bhakti* appears in the *Śvetāśvatara Upaniṣad* as mentioned earlier.

First signs of personal *bhakti* appear in the epic period. The stories of devotion of Lakṣmaṇa, Bharata and Hanumān to Rāma in the *Rāmāyaṇa* stand out as examples of selfless surrender. In the *Mahābhārata*, Arjuna is projected as the *śakhā-bhakta* of Kṛṣṇa. In the *Bhagavadgītā*, subtext of the *Mahābhārata*, *bhakti* appears as *bhakti-yoga*. In south India, the two epics that extant are: *Cilappadikaram* and *Maṇimekhalai*. We find rudimentary references of devotion in the *Cilappadikaram*, at least at two places. First is the episode of enactment of round-dance of cow-herd girls with Pinnai (Rādhā) at the centre, this episode echoes Rāsalīlā of the *Bhāgavata Purāṇa* which is considered to be the pinnacle of self-surrender in *bhakti*. The second is the enactment of Kannagi's demand for justice where she burnt the city of Madurai but calmed down at the behest of Goddess Mīnākṣī and later was regarded a goddess herself.

The wave of *bhakti* originated in the Tamil land in south India where *bhakti* as a form of devotion to personal god was popularized by the Nāyanmār and the Āḷvār saints, who flourished between sixth and tenth centuries. Due to the strong influence of these Śaiva and Vaiṣṇava saints, respectively, *bhakti* became a popular practice mode of experiencing the higher realms of consciousness. Ordinary people followed these itinerant saints like charmed spirits. These saints wandered singing their own devotional compositions throughout the land. Wherever they went they transformed the small locus of regional/village deities into sacred space of pilgrimage (*tīrtha*) of high importance. Their presence outside of temple space and their singing in vernacular tongues overturned the supremacy of classical *bhakti* that was marked by Brāhmanical and Sanskrit's linguistic dominance, Sanskrit being the language of Brāhmanical ritualism. These wandering saints in a way democratized *bhakti* by making it an experience accessible to all groups of society regardless of caste, class, gender, religion. Women, children, rich, poor, brāhmaṇa, kṣatriya, vaiśya or śūdra – all could connect with their impassioned expression and to the emotional thrust of their compositions. This took the edge away from the temple space as well as from the scriptural authority. Now the emphasis was put upon the idea of body itself as the temple and a pure heart that sang in love and blissful ecstasy. This kind of devotional love brought about a shift from ritual space of the temple to the mystical space of the heart of the devotee. It also allowed for authentic experience of unification with higher consciousness by removing the dualism between devotee and temple or God – now the devotee's heart itself has turned into a hermitage of God.

Medieval Bhakti

Classical form of *bhakti* paved the way for turning *bhakti* into a widespread movement in medieval period. The sentiment of devotion to a personal god spread like forest fire and took the whole country in its grip by the end of fifteenth century. The most significant shift in devotional paradigm happened in this period when the object of devotion (personal god) moved from its official dwelling space of the temple to a home in the heart space of the devotee. *Bhakti* movement also nourished a lot of small reform movements with reference to issues of gender, caste, class and politics. It also contributed to the development of regional languages. Starting in south in sixth century, it spread from Tamil land to Maharashtra, Bengal, Assam, Uttar Pradesh and by fourteenth century it spread in the entire subcontinent.

Medieval *bhakti* movement created a pan-Indian wave of devotional energy that enveloped Indian subcontinent for hundreds of years and left its influence on other religious streams as well. Under the influence of *bhakti*, individual *bhakta*s often stood strong against dominating religious institutions and hierarchies of caste, class and gender. They lived a love-intoxicated life and created new standards of morality, ethics and compassion. Their lived experiences were regarded with deep reverence and set examples for generations to follow. Well-known saints like Karaikal Ammaiyar, Āṇḍāl, Basavanna, Allamā Prabhu, Akkā Mahādevī, Sant Jñāneśvar, Sant Nāmdev, Caitanya Mahāprabhu, Śaṅkaradeva, Pūran Dāsa, Mīrābāī, Kabīr, Tulsīdās, Sūrdās, Ramakrishna Paramahamsa, Ramaṇa Maharṣi – all lived an exemplary life and revealed the limitations of orthodox religion and the oppressive casteist social norms and customs associated with it. They addressed the existing socio-religious limitations in different ways in their compositions, teachings and/or writings. Many of these devotees/saints had to face strong social and religious opposition for different reasons at different times. Yet they stood firm on their path. Their life episodes and the values by which they lived proved to be far higher than the socio-religious morality and ethics which bind an ordinary person to a limited plane of awareness.

Modern Bhakti

In modern times, devotional love has broken out of religious paraphernalia – its expression has been renewed and redefined in various ways. Modern sages and spiritual masters have indicated that expression of loving devotion is not a prerogative of any particular religion, it can be practised even without a belief in a particular 'god'. This creates a shift in the perspective which has hitherto trapped *bhakti* in religious outfit. The devotional love in this new perspective has turned into an intense method for transforming lower human emotions and channelling them into an all-embracing higher emotion of loving coexistence.

Modern spiritual masters like Swami Sivananda Saraswati of Divine Life Society, Rishikesh; Swami Satyananda Saraswati; Swami Niranjanananda Saraswati; Swami Satyasangananda Saraświti of Bihar School of Yoga, Munger; Ma Anandamayi; Swami Rama of Himalayan Institute; Acharya Rajneesh "Osho", Mata Amritanandamayi and Sadguru Sri Jaggi Vasudev of Isha Foundation, Sri Sri Ravishankar of Art of Living – all of them involve with devotion and present it in such a way that it takes a leap over religion. Swami Satyananda Saraswati very aptly explains that *bhakti* is not a ritualistic or religious path:

> The path of devotion is the path of *bhakti-yoga*, but *bhakti* should not be understood in the religious sense. Religion and *bhakti* are not the same and when you practise a religion, you do not necessarily practise *bhakti*.
>
> . . . *Bhakti* can easily be labelled a blind dogma and in many cases it has degenerated into exactly this. In the past and in the present day, *Bhakti* has been totally misunderstood and misused. This has led to fanaticism and intolerance. This is not what *bhakti* is all about. *Bhakti* is not something that is easily acceptable to the modern intellectual world. Yet, this is a great pity, for *bhakti-yoga* is an incredibly powerful method that can lead to higher knowledge and

> transcendence. Not only this, *bhakti-yoga* can help you harmonize your life and make life the joy that it should be.
>
> . . .
>
> *Bhakti* is an intense awareness of the object of love. This love and attachment is not intellectual, not merely ritualistic, not just an expression of a particular cult. It is a part of your being. You do not have to learn how to love, how to practise attachment. They are already in you. . . . The practice of *bhakti* is mind consuming. It is such a powerful path! Once you can handle it, awakening is just a joke, but if you understand *bhakti* as prayer, rituals, reading of scriptures or just talking about God, then you have missed the point. – 1991, *Sayings of a Paramahansa*.

Swami Niranjananada Saraswati, an enlightened modern sage, describes devotion as a lifestyle, an art of living. He says: "There are many beliefs about *bhakti*; however, *bhakti* is a lifestyle, an art of living. . . . "

A modern scholar of Vaiṣṇava *bhakti*, David Haberman describes *bhakti* as "a contemplative technique that both utilizes and generates emotion" (Haberman 2001: 65).

A modern saint and a mystic, Sadguru Jaggi Vasudev (2017) describes devotion even as a type of intelligence. According to him:

> Devotion is another dimension of Intelligence. Devotion is intelligence, you understand, is bigger intelligence and when you have learnt to keep your little intellect aside – that is devotion. Devotion does not mean doing *pūjā* everyday. Devotion simply means your involvement with life is so absolute that even you don't matter anymore. Your involvement with what you have taken up is so absolute that who you are does not matter – then you are a devotee. Devotion means you are devoid of yourself – that is devotion.

Swami Satyananda and Sadguru Jaggi Vasudev in the above quotations are talking about one of the most important ingredients of devotion – elimination of the limited self. It is in this context that Sage Nārada's *Bhaktisūtra* serves a useful purpose with its depiction of techniques that help one overcome the limited egotistical self.

Part I

1

Devotional Love Beyond Religion

EXISTENTIAL questions for human race have been same since the advent of the civilization. We pursued and attained unimaginable success in the realm of earthly existence. However, we only encountered dissatisfaction, discontentment, despair and endless yearning for 'more' in the external world. Surprisingly, this yearning refuses to be gratified even if we feed it with 'more'. Wise sages who understood this endless cycle of desire and gratification explored a counter space which was the inner space of the individual self. They realized that in the inner space, there were immense possibilities for contentment, joy and peace without much effort. They, then, laid down their experiences as teachings to help others who desired to look beyond what was perceivable to the senses. These teachings or tools are available in all cultures, sometimes hidden, sometimes visible and accessible. In India, these teachings are more visible because they have been kept alive within the tradition. These teachings are the seeds of self-realization. Human consciousness is the soil on which these seeds can grow and bear fruit. It is obvious that it is our own consciousness which is the source of our joys as well as our sorrows, but unfortunately we do not have access to the whole range of our consciousness. Unless we apply ourselves in a disciplined manner to inner self-exploration, we cannot have access to the full range of our consciousness. We cannot easily fathom what lies in the subconscious and the unconscious part of our being. Most of us work only from the limited part of the conscious mind throughout our lives thereby living a discontented or half-fulfilling life.

Ancient sages found out that if we could have access to the entire range of our consciousness, we could become free from the cycles of suffering and joy. They also found out that we are inter-sewn with the whole creation with a single thread. We are a part of a super-consciousness which is all-pervading; complete and absolute. This has been termed as Supreme Consciousness. This all-pervading consciousness envelops all beings in the creation. It includes all existents – plants, trees, animals, rivers, birds, mountains, oceans, etc. Human beings can experience this unity with the whole creation only when they are able to expand the range of their awareness in such a way that they have access to all the dimensions of their consciousness. In other words, the individual becomes one with the whole cosmos and feels complete and contented only if s/he can actually access/experience the whole range of his/her consciousness. The *Bṛhadāraṇyaka Upaniṣad* talks about this state of completeness in a *mantra* which is a popular chant recited after the culmination of many sacred rituals:

> ॐ पूर्णमदः पूर्णमिदं पूर्णात्पूर्णमुदच्यते ।
> पूर्णस्य पूर्णमादाय पूर्णमेवावशिष्यते ॥
>
> *oṁ pūrṇamadaḥ pūrṇamidaṁ pūrṇātpūrṇamudacyate* ।
> *pūrṇasya pūrṇamādāya pūrṇamevāvaśiṣyate* ॥
>
> That is full, this is full. From the full, full only arises. When fullness is taken out of fullness, fullness only remains.

This *mantra* suggests a level of awareness in which the seeker (*bhakta*) has attained complete contentment and is able to experience harmony with every aspect of creation.

In the light of the above description, we may clearly say that *bhakti* or loving devotion has been/can be one method amongst many others that allows us to participate in the fullness of life. With careful analysis, we can see that *bhakti* can serve as an effective tool of internalization and focus that felicitates entry into those parts of our consciousness which are otherwise hidden from our conscious faculties.

Devotion as All-Embracing Love

Ancient sages devised tools to attain the state of completeness as mentioned above. This completeness is also termed as enlightenment or self-realization in the spiritual discourse. To attain a state of enlightenment there has to be an expansion in the normal state of consciousness with which most of us live in our earthly existence. This expansion can either be gradual or can be a sudden explosion like the *kuṇḍalinī* awakening. The latter can be literally compared to a sudden lighting up of a thousand light bulbs in our brain cells. It is scientifically proven that we use only a minuscule of our brain's full potential. We may say that complete lighting in our consciousness is equivalent to our brain becoming fully active. Hence, what the sages called as 'enlightenment' may also be called as 'full realization of our human potential'. As to the process of enlightenment and how it can be achieved, the sages gave us numerous methods and practice tools which may lead us to enlightenment. Each of these practice tools is as unique and efficient as the other because each one of them is based on concrete personal experience of one or the other realized master.

For a modern seeker these practice tools are available in unprecedented abundance. Modern technology has made available this special knowledge which in earlier times was considered esoteric and was transferred only in *gurū–śiṣya* lineage (master–disciple tradition). At the same time, when we look closely we see that all these tools have something in common, something essentially basic which makes them all work for the same result, i.e. enlightenment or realization of our full potential. The benefit of this variety is that each one of us can have a practice path which is most suitable to our natural inclinations. However, in spite of this enormity of information, need for a spiritual master is unequivocally emphasized in all the sacred traditions for a serious seeker on the spiritual path. Without the grace and guidance of a realized master, the seeker may miss the whole point of life.

Bhakti is said to be the easiest path or easiest tool to attain a state of completeness. The reason for *bhakti* being easy for human beings may lie in the fact that human beings are the only creatures who are capable of expressing intense emotions. Modern researchers have confirmed that human beings are emotional beings and that our actions are motivated more by our emotions than by our considered opinions and thoughts. One of the most overpowering emotions in all humans is that of love. Love is the finest mystery as well as a miracle in creation. It is that aspect of being which is inexplicable and yet is the only aspect of being which allows life to continue in all forms. All forms in creation are born out of love and live in search of love only. *Bhakti* is this same love but it is a love that embraces all including even that which is not visible to naked eye. It is a special type of love which should not be considered superstitious. We may say that a special all-inclusive love experienced at its height is *bhakti*.

Bhakti as love is expansive in nature. It allows for an expansion in our emotional energy field which in turn effects an all-embracing acceptance of life in all its forms and formulations. In other words, when human love becomes expansive enough to embrace all the existence, it automatically turns into *bhakti*. *Bhakti* is love in its fullness and in this sense, it is supreme love. Ancient sages, seers and *yogīs* perceived and revealed to their disciples that energy of love is very powerful in humans. They revealed how only human beings can transform the energy of all their lower emotions like anger, fear, jealousy, etc. into the energy of supreme love. Sage Nārada's *Bhaktisūtra* is part of such a revelation.

Practice of *bhakti* as a tool to transform limited human love into all-embracing supreme love can also be taken up in a systematic manner. Then it becomes *bhakti-yoga* – a discipline of love. Amongst various examples of *bhakti-yoga* practised in and around India, one of the best examples is seen in Bihar School of Yoga Tradition. Swami Niranjanananda Saraswati, the present Paramācārya of Bihar School of Yoga interpreted his Parama Guru Swami Sivananda Saraswati's eightfold teachings as a very subtle form of eightfold *yoga* (*aṣṭāṅga-yoga*) which, according to him, is the most adequate form of practice for the modern seekers. This modern *aṣṭāṅga* discipline is a step higher to Sage Patañjali's *aṣṭāṅga-yoga*. While in Patañjali's yogic discipline, the eight stages are *yama, niyama, āsana, prāṇāyāma, pratyāhāra, dhāraṇā, dhyāna* and *samādhi*, the *aṣṭāṅga-yoga* given by Swami Sivananda and exposited by Swami Niranjanananda is: Serve, Love, Give, Meditate, Be Good, Do Good, Be Kind and Be Compassionate.[1] It is worth the mention here that the Rikhiapeeth Ashram of the same tradition puts to practice Swami Sivananda's *aṣṭāṅga-yoga* (rightfold discipline). The very theme of life at this Ashram is "Serve, Love, Give" which is the highest form of *bhakti-yoga*. Acts of "service,

---

1 These teachings have been adapted as a song and are sung in the lineage of Swami Sivananda Saraswati. The composition is easily available on Youtube: "serve, love, give, purify, meditate, realise/be good, do good, be kind, be compassionate/enquire who am I, know thyself and be free/bear insult, bear injury highest *sādhanā*".

compassion and giving" automatically purify the individual consciousness in such a way that unconditional love flowers on its own in this consciousness. And unconditional love with egoless attitude is *bhakti* which works as the quickest aid to experience and live an enlightened state of consciousness.

Devotion for Focus and to Attain Higher States of Consciousness

As has been said earlier, the idea of existence of God is very helpful but not necessary in *bhakti*. The path and the process of *bhakti* involves ability to love unconditionally. The idea of God as all-pervasive serves as an excellent object for this kind of love. Many cultures across the world have delineated God in human form because this helps in focusing the awareness easily. Focus on a chosen form is the main component in the *bhakti* method of self-realization. In fact, amongst all the ways available for enlightenment, the main emphasis is on development of 'one-pointed focus'. It is only after the seeker has developed a sharp mental focus that an expansion (actually an explosion) in the awareness takes place. Expansion in the awareness lights up the whole range of consciousness – conscious, subconscious and unconscious – thereby effecting the manifestation of full human potential in an individual.

Different traditions use different symbols for developing mental focus. Buddhists for instance use breath as an object to practise focus; tāntrics use *mantras*, *yantras* and *maṇḍalas* to practise focus; *yogīs* practise alignment of *manas-śakti* and *prāṇa-śakti* to attain concentration and focus; *bhaktas* use the image of their chosen god (*iṣṭa*) to practise one-pointedness. In this way, a non-believer may like to choose his/her own secular symbol as a practice tool for attaining one-pointedness. In classical *bhakti*, 'God' is the symbol. Due to the emotional energy that the devotee directs towards God, it becomes a very real phenomenon for his/her. By and by the whole world becomes God's body for the devotee and all that happens in the world happens through the energy in that body.

Devotion to Transform Lower Emotions into Supreme Love

Human beings have strong emotions. Some of us are able to use them to our advantage; others suppress them and in turn become depressed. Suppressed emotions take the form of physical or mental illnesses. Awakened beings believe that if these emotions are not directed or channelled, they become the bane of our life. Swami Satyasangananda Saraswati, a disciple of Swami Satyananda Saraswati, has talked about solo form of energy (in Tantra it is called Śakti) which is behind all human emotions, be they positive or negative. In human beings, the negative emotions like anger, hatred, jealousy, greed, irritability and fear coexist with compassion, cooperation, enthusiasm, happiness, need for sharing and for love. The direction that this energy takes depends upon an individual's level of awareness. Same energy can flow in positive or in negative direction. Renowned Vietnamese monk Thich Naht Hanh has often remarked that if we make a conscious choice to water and nourish only the positive emotions in life and to not water the negative ones, then all negativity in us will slowly dry up. The path of *bhakti* provides the water which nourishes our positive emotions.

2

Contemporary Relevance of Devotion as Selfless Love

THERE is a popular mythological story about *daityas* (demons) and *devatās* (divine beings) who were invited to a feast in the heavenly abode of Lord Viṣṇu. Once Lord Viṣṇu wanted these beings to know of their real nature. He decided to invite them for a feast. On the day of the feast two big halls of exactly same nature were decorated and set up to welcome the two groups. The greatest of chefs were engaged to create delicacies for them. Both the groups were directed to the halls meant for them. Soon both the parties found themselves seated on long tables with two rows of chairs facing each other. The tables were filled with choicest foods from heavenly kitchen and the aroma rising from different foods served to whet the appetite of guests. With his super powers Lord Viṣṇu appeared simultaneously in both the halls. After everyone chanted the prayers, Lord Viṣṇu gave the green signal for the feast to begin. But lo and behold! The Lord did a trick with demons as well as with divine beings. He straightened their hands at the elbow so that no one could bend their elbows. Imagine eating without bending the elbow. It is impossible. The hungry guests were utterly surprised. What kind of an invitation is this! One is served the best of foods but cannot eat it and the host is just smiling mischievously at their misery.

However, after some time the scenario in the two halls was quite a spectacle. In the hall where the demons were seated, the whole place turned into an animal shed. As the demons, now unable to bend their elbows and take the food into their mouth, began to put their mouth into the pots in an effort to eat whatever they could. The containers turned upside down. The food got spread all over. Food went into their eyes and nose and spread all over their faces. Their clothes also got smeared. In fact, they could hardly eat. There was only chaos, quarrel and helplessness. Lord Viṣṇu was watching the whole scene still with his famous smile. Presently, the head of the demons asked him in desperation "Why do you play your tricks on us? What wrong have we done, now?", Lord Viṣṇu patiently asked the demon head to follow him to the other hall where the *devatā*s, the divine beings, were seated.

Here, the scenario was completely different. The head of demons witnessed that the *devatā*s also could not bend their elbows and could not bring the food that lay on the table in front of them to their mouth. Yet each was eating happily and was enjoying the delicious food from God's own kitchen. There was no chaos, no noise, no spilling – just harmonious joy. What he saw was beyond his imagination. He saw that each *devatā* was feeding the *devatā* seated opposite to him on the table. They could not bend their elbows but they could reach the food to the other *devatā* with their straight arm. They were lovingly feeding each other and in turn were able to enjoy the feast to the full in spite of the limitation put on them by God.

The head of demons was awakened to a new understanding.

He understood that Lord Viṣṇu wanted to show him and his community what is it that they can improve in their nature in order to live a more beautiful, fulfilling and harmonious life.

They just have to put the other's interest before their

personal interest. They just have to make a 180 degree turn to arrive at the hall of divine beings and leave behind their demonic fellowship by a single-minded decision to think of their fellow beings before thinking about their own self.

It is selfless surrender that loving devotion is all about. And, lest we should get afraid that selfless love means personal deprivation or self-erasure, we should be clear that it is rather the opposite. We just need some kind of contemplative moments that give us patience to realize that we are not isolated beings but that each of us is a part of us. *Bhakti* is one of the methods that reaches us at that point of realization. *Bhakti* (selfless love) creates the understanding that our personal cravings can be satisfied in a better way if we first take into account of the needs of our fellow beings.

We witness social unrest in all parts of the world with exploitative political agendas leading to economic imbalance, environmental degradation and exploitation of natural resources leading to climate change. The whole life on the planet has become prone to disease, deprivation and violence. As a reaction to this an undercurrent of awareness is on the rise which makes it very clear to modern individual, now than ever before, that humanity must learn to survive with much less greed and more equalized consumption. Many individuals who are aware of this and many groups/ communities who believe in alternate ways of living have voluntarily chosen to live frugally and are bravely defying thoughtless consumerism. Many have started their combat by making exemplary moves towards a life of non-possession (*aparigraha*) and non-greed. This awareness can slowly sieve down into mainstream cultures as well.

At the same time, it is significant to note that since antiquity the Asian cultures, particularly the Indian culture, have treasured communities of wanderers (*sādhu*s), monks (*bhikkhus*) and renunciants (*saṁnyāsins*) who voluntarily chose a frugal lifestyle and which has been kept alive in the monastery and hermitage (*āśrama*) traditions. These monks and renunciants have been the torchbearers for people living in the clutches of consumerism. The householders and people living in mainstream looked up to them for guidance and for secrets of harmonious and happy living. Even in modern times, inhabitants of these *āśrama*s and monasteries inspire a fulfilling lifestyles to others who are consumed by fast-changing times.

The attitude of devotion or selfless surrender removes the egotism from our emotional energy field. It gives us patience which in turn expands our understanding of a larger reality. Selfless persons are the ones who are truly devotional. Selfless service to others in any form and *bhakti* or devotional surrender to God are two names of the same phenomenon. Thus, if an individual is able to navigate through life without self-centred egotism, then we may say that he/she is a real devotee of the Supreme and that s/he is living a fulfilling life at many other planes than just the sensual, emotional, mental or intellectual planes on which most of us presently live.

3

Nārada Bhakti Sūtra[1]

A Reading

THE NĀRADA BHAKTI SŪTRA text is a compilation of eighty-four aphorisms. The number 84 is significant as it reminds of Hindu belief that a soul gets a human body only after passing through 84,000 different births (*yonis*). Human body is special because only human beings are capable of experiencing and attaining higher states of consciousness. This text is about a simple way described as devotional love to experience those states of consciousness. Author of this text is named as Nārada as is suggested in its last aphorism. However, it is debatable whether Sage Nārada was the author of this text. The text was compiled in eleventh century CE. It can be easily conjectured that the aphorisms as such are not coming directly to us from Sage Nārada who is mentioned in the Purāṇas as an immortal being who wanders through the three worlds. This text may have been put together by

[1] The word *sūtra* in the title appears differently in different versions of the text. Some writers like Swami Vivekananda use *Nārada-Bhakti-sūtra* and others like Swami Bhuteshananda and Swami Prabhavananda use *Nārada-Bhaktisūtras* in the title.

Nārada Bhakti Sūtra with *sūtra* as a singular word is more appropriate because *sūtra* is literally one single thread which binds many components together like beads in a rosary. The individual phrases within the text may be called "aphorisms". However in all the available English translations of this text each aphorism is referred to as *sūtra* which then makes the text a collection of *sūtras*.

I have kept the title as *Nārada Bhakti Sūtra* but I also use the word *sūtra* for each aphorism for the sake of convenience.

a medieval scholar and *bhakta*, who was deeply inspired by the character and personality of Sage Nārada. The author apotheosized Nārada because Sage Nārada is considered to be one of the supreme *bhakta*s.

In other words, it could also be said that Nārada of antiquity is not the author of this text but the inspirer of the text and that an unknown person compiled the aphorisms on *bhakti* that were prevailing in the name of Nārada's teachings on *bhakti*. He might have structured the text on the basis of what he considered to be the most essential teachings of Nārada. This compiler may have received the idea of *bhakti* as a course of devotion from the hagiography of Sage Nārada and may have expounded it for the benefit of his students and others. Another conjecture is that there was a *Bhaktisūtra* composed by Sage Nārada and that it came down in oral form to succeeding generations until it was put together by this eleventh-century compiler.

The aphorisms in the *sūtra* are very simple dictations on the idea and practice of devotion as found in the classical tradition. As the aphorisms mention *gopikā*s' love for Kṛṣṇa in detail, it is clear that they were compiled later than the *Bhāgavatam*. The text could have been compiled in or after eleventh century CE, before the Muslim conquest of north India (1193–1203) and much after the documentation of the *Bhāgavata Purāṇa*. To quote from an essay on *bhakti* period from *Sacred Sanskrit Literature*:

> The *Nārada Bhakti Sūtra* and the *Śāṇḍilya Bhakti Sūtra* are brief compendiums of the *bhakti* system, probably meant to be committed to memory by ascetics. Both are clearly dependent on the *Bhāgavata*, and neither mentions Rādhā. The *Nārada* is simple both in language and thought, and is practical in aim; . . . – Kapoor 2002: 462

Although the simplicity of teachings prescribed in the text

makes this text very popular and accesible but its simplicity also posits some limitations.

The *Nārada Bhakti Sūtra* is embedded in the *vaidhi bhakti* line of Vaiṣṇava *bhakti* tradition which is the preparation stage for the higher *rāgānuga bhakti* in which devotion arises spontaneously due to passionate love for the Supreme. In *vaidhi* path the instructions of the scriptures have to be strictly followed until the loving devotion becomes natural. Thus the *Nārada Bhakti Sūtra* appears more to be a book of instructions rather than one which gives insights into higher states of consciousness where the individual consciousness merges with the Cosmic Consciousness or Supreme Consciousness.

There are only fleeting indications about the dissolution of limited consciousness into the expansive Cosmic Consciousness that is attainable by devotion. A few instances occur in *sūtra* 4, *yallabdhvā pumān;... sūtra* 6, *ātmārāmo bhavati* and in *sūtra* 41, *tasmiṁstajjane bhedābhāvāt*. Nārada hints that at such a state of consciousness, where the devotee gets established in the Self, becomes one with the Self, and attains a state in which there is no difference between God and the devotee.

The *Nārada Bhakti Sūtra*, being a popular text from eleventh century, does not mention the Āgamic non-dual (Advaita) form of devotion which prevailed in Kashmir and which was strengthed by the ninth-century Kashmir Śaiva master Utpaladeva in his *Śiva-Stotrāvalī*.

Nārada in the Tradition

Sage Nārada is a very significant figure in Indian spiritual tradition. Sometimes he appears to be many figures who merge into one figure of a supreme *bhakta* wandering in the universe chanting the name of God since antiquity.[2] This

[2] *Brahmavaivarta Purāṇa* (chaps 19-30) describe episodes of Nārada's birth, his life and his devotional love.

image survived in the mass consciousness till date.

Swami Tyagishananda in his commentary on the *Nārada Bhakti Sūtra* gives an elaborate description of the character of Nārada through the ages. According to him:

> Nārada is the divine messenger in the Purāṇas, nay, the friend, philosopher, guide and consoler of all – gods, men and demons – the intermediary between God and his creation.

In the *Ṛgveda*, the name 'Nārada' is attributed to a seer of a hymn. He is also considered to be one of the sons of Brahmā.

In the Purāṇas, Nārada is considered to be the greatest devotee of God. He has been conferred with immortality by Lord Viṣṇu and now wanders through the cosmos singing the names of 'Nārāyaṇa'. 'Nārāyaṇa' is form of God Viṣṇu and Nārada's aphorisms fall in the tradition of Vaiṣṇava *bhakti*.

In the *Vālmīki Rāmāyaṇa*, it is Nārada who recounts the story of Rāma to Sanatkumāra. Sage Vālmīki begins this great epic with an address to Nārada. The first *śloka* of Bālakāṇḍa of *Vālmīki Rāmāyaṇa* ascribes to Sage Nārada the highest virtues of a *yogī* and a renunciant *bhakta*:

> ॐ तपःस्वाध्यायनिरतं तपस्वी वाग्विदां वरम् ।
> नारदं परिपप्रच्छ वाल्मीकिर्मुनिपुंगवम् ।।
>
> *oṁ tapaḥsvādhyāyaniratam tapasvī vāgvidāṁ varam* ।
> *nāradaṁ paripapṛccha vālmīkirmunipuṅgavam* ।।
>
> Sage Nārada, who was the greatest among the renunciants engaged in ascetic practices and in the study of the Self, Vālmīki asked him thus. . . .

At one place, the *Bhāgavata Purāṇa* mentions 'Nārada' as the third *avatāra* among the twenty-one *avatāra*s of Viṣṇu and at another place he is mentioned as son of a maid-servant who becomes immortal due to his devotion and due to God's grace (Swami Tyagishananda 2001).

At least three other texts besides the *Bhaktisūtra* have been ascribed to Nārada but it can't be said whether these texts were written by the same person. These texts are *Nāradasmṛti*, *Nāradīyaśikṣā* and *Saṅgītamakaranda* (Tyagishananda 2001).

Sūtra as a Form of Transmission

In ancient Sanskrit literature, *sūtra* was a popular form of transmission of knowledge in the *guru–śiṣya* tradition. It must have been an excellent method of teaching at the time when all one could depend on was memory. *Sūtra* refers to a series of aphorisms or concise phrases, each consisting of minimum number of words to express a particular doctrine, which could be easily memorized. *Sūtra* literally means 'thread' and the *sūtra* texts were written on palm leaves sewn together with a thread. Aphorisms in a *sūtra* text are characterized by brevity and precision of expression. The disciple could learn the *sūtra*s by heart and could contemplate over the content in the time ascribed for *svādhyāya* (self-study). Ācārya Pāṇini's Sanskrit grammar *Aṣṭādhyāyī* with 4,000 aphorisms is the finest example of *sūtra* form where this form is put to its most effective use in the history of Sanskrit language and literature. Many philosophical doctrines were committed to *sūtra* form in the ancient and pre-medieval period. Dharmasūtras, Gṛhyasūtras, *Brahmasūtra*, *Bhaktisūtra*, *Yogasūtra* and *Śivasūtra* are some of the famous treatises composed in *sūtra* form.

Relevance of the Bhaktisūtra

The most important concept in the *Nārada Bhakti Sūtra* is the idea that *bhakti* (loving devotion) creates a predisposition for unconditional love in the seeker or the devotee. Next important concept is the need for dissolution of individual self on the path of *bhakti*. Obsession with the individual self is a growing menace in modern existence – the cause of which lies in our ego-centrism. The *Nārada Bhakti Sūtra* teaches us to surrender the ego to gain a higher kind of energy. The text lays emphasis on the need on part of the seeker to transform his/her basic emotions like greed, pride, jealousy and anger, singularly into an emotion of unconditional compassion for everyone and everything in the creation.

Although the subject matter of the *Nārada Bhakti Sūtra* is based on classical *bhakti*, his aphorisms are quite relevant in the present context because if we sift these aphorisms out of their religious vocabulary and place them in the realm of the spiritual, then a modern seeker can also learn from them the art of living a life of love and cooperation.

In terms of content, the text of *Nārada Bhakti Sūtra* is simple. It appears to lure, initiate and guide a devotional student/seeker to walk on the path of loving devotion. The sage promises that the path of *bhakti* is the easiest amongst the other prescribed paths to attain the Supreme and that the practice of loving devotion will help them to arrive at a destination which is very high. He begins with giving a very appealing definition of devotion, saying that "*Bhakti* is highest love for the highest, the Supreme. This love is without attribute, unconditional, unceasing, ever-increasing and is very subtle" (*sūtra*s 2 and 51-54). Then he goes on to describe the blissful tranquillity of mind and the mystical powers that a sincere devotee gains with *bhakti* (*sūtra*s 3-6 and 60). Then he describes the manners of being that help on the path of loving devotion. The most primary discipline is the single-minded attentiveness for the object of love, the Supreme (*sūtra* 7). Nārada says that harmonious actions in the world lead to the required single-minded focus (*sūtra* 8). This focus is strengthened by uninterrupted remembrance of the

Supreme and by repudiating gregariousness and indulgence in sense objects (*sūtras* 35-36). In order to sustain the focus, wrong or inappropriate company must be relegated and the company of truth and truthful should be sought because the wrong company feeds lower emotions of anger, lust and delusion, and leads to memory loss and total annihilation (*sūtras* 43-44). In a very poetic aphorism, Nārada explains that the vices which are initially like ephemeral waves turn into a big ocean under the influence of a bad company or bad social engagement (*sūtra* 45). Further, he commands that the devotee must drop pride and arrogance from his/her nature.

The sage then talks about the features of a good devotee. A good devotee is single-minded in devotion (*sūtra* 67). He/she does not discriminate on the basis of caste, class, colour, gender, etc. (*sūtra* 72). The person doesn't waste time in unnecessary arguments, rather contemplates over the teachings of the path. The devotee's actions are guided by loving devotion (*sūtra* 76). He/she should not waste even a moment without awareness of the Supreme and should wait eagerly for the time when state of equanimity and bliss will dawn upon him/her (*sūtra* 77).

An individual should practise the rules of cleanliness, contentment, non-violence and compassion in order to live harmoniously in his/her social space (*sūtra* 78).

The central aphorism of the text perhaps is *sūtra* 82 where the sage describes methods of devotion in his elevenfold devotional ways (*ekādaśadhā bhakti*). Here, he says that although devotion is singular, it can be executed in eleven ways. The devotee may choose to focus on the virtues and characteristic features of his/her chosen deity, on the visual form, on the loving offering, on constant remembrance, on being at service continually, on being a close friend, on being the beloved, on being a mother or a father, on total surrender of the self, on being identical with the Supreme and finally on painful separation from the loved one, the Supreme. The Supreme can be conceived in a form which is most appealing to the devotee.

These ways of elevenfold devotion were later subsumed into the ninefold devotional ways made famous through the *Bhāgavata Purāṇa*. These methods of expressing love for the Supreme by forging an emotional relationship with that principle are easy and an ordinary human consciousness can access them. No extra wisdom or intellect or any other special qualification is needed to engage in loving devotion to that invisible power.

The chief instructions given in the *Nārada Bhakti Sūtra* to develop and maintain the devotional love to attain the Supreme (beloved) can be summarized in following points:

1. What is *bhakti* (devotion)? It is absolute love for the Supreme.
2. When this loving devotion is perfected, then one rises above the realm of sorrows and joys, becomes completely content and forever enjoys relishing the Self. Devotion gives such a sense of fulfilment within that no desire is left to be fulfilled in the outside world.
3. Loving devotion liberates one from desires in the world and also from prescriptions of scriptures for living.
4. Absolute focus is absorption in One in exclusion to all else. There should be total indifference to everything else which is not that or is against that One.
5. In devotion, one offers one's self completely to the Supreme through reverence, through remembrance and through seeing the Supreme in one's own self.
6. Excessive indulgence in sense objects should be

watched, excessive need for company should be pruned.

7. Loving devotion to Supreme can be attained through unceasing contemplation.
8. Singing *kīrtana* in gathering of like-minded leads to perfection in devotion to Supreme.
9. Perfection in devotional love can be attained mainly by grace or by blessings of the great saints who are rare.
10. Bad company should be renounced at all costs because even a figment of lower emotions of anger, lust, etc. can become big like a mountain under the influence of wrong company.
11. One who becomes detached from the fruit of actions and transcends duality achieves liberation.
12. Devotional love is without attributes, without expectations, i.e. it is unconditional. It keeps on increasing every moment. It is very subtle and it is within the range of human experience.
13. Loving devotion leads to peace and deep joy.
14. Devotees do not discriminate on the basis of caste, class or colour. They don't engage in unnecessary arguments. They don't waste time but use it in remembrance of the Supreme.
15. They should always follow the principles of non-violence, truth, cleanliness, faith and mercy or compassion.
16. Loving devotion can be expressed through emotional bonding with the object of love.

There can be many ways of developing an emotional relation. The eleven ways are:

a. Immerse in love for the virtues and qualities of chosen deity.
b. Immerse in love for the visual form of the chosen deity or chosen object of love.
c. Immerse in love by way of giving loving offerings to the deity.
d. Immerse in love through constant remembrance of the loved One.
e. Immerse in love as if one is a servant and is constantly at service of the deity or God or loved one.
f. Immerse in love like a very close friend of God.
g. Immerse in love like a lover or beloved of the deity or God.
h. Immerse in love like a mother or a father of deity or God.
i. Surrender the self completely and accept workings of Higher Will.
j. Develop a sense of identity or oneness with the chosen deity or God.
k. Become immersed in love which is felt at the time of separation from a loved one.

In conclusion, we can say that the *Nārada Bhakti Sūtra* is a manual of instructions for the uninitiated. Its value lies in the way it knocks at the storehouse of human emotions and describes the ways in which emotions can be used to create a strong relationship with the intangible Supreme Energy pervading and enveloping the universe.

Part II

Nārada Bhakti Sūtra
The Aphorisms

One

Definition of Bhakti

1

अथातो भक्तिं व्याख्यास्यामः

athāto bhaktiṁ vyākhyāsyāmaḥ ।

Now, hereafter, we shall describe *bhakti*.

Interpretation: Sage Nārada begins his work in the traditional *sūtra* style. *Sūtra* form has been a very popular mode of instruction in ancient times when the teaching was imparted orally. Precision and memorability of expression were aspects of prime significance in an oral learning culture. The aphorisms in *sūtra*, being short, pithy and poetic phrases, were very easy to memorize. Therefore they could be effortlessly relegated to a disciple's memory. Consequently, they could also be easily preserved in *guru–śiṣya* tradition from one generation to the other. An important aspect of *sūtra* texts is that each aphorism in the text is connected to the next one and to the whole theme in such a way that the subject under enquiry can be exposited from beginning to the end in all its dimensions.

In this first *sūtra*, Nārada introduces the subject and the theme of his composition. Then he moves on to explicate other dimensions of the subject. Sage Patañjali also begins his *Yogasūtra* in the same manner. First *yogasūtra* is: *atha yoga anuśāsanam* (अथ योगानुशासनम्).

2

सा त्वस्मिन् परमप्रेमरूपा ।।

sā tvasmin pramapremarūpā ।।

That (*bhakti*) in this (context) is of the form of supreme love.

Interpretation: Sage Nārada gives a concise definition of *bhakti* in this *sūtra* and describes it as having the form of highest love. The word *asmin* (in this) may indicate Nārada's emphasis on a particular context in which he places his subject. He must be aware of other contexts in which *bhakti* can be studied.

In this *sūtra*, the sage specifies that the highest love is *bhakti*. Love at its zenith becomes *bhakti*. Whether it is love for other human beings or for other forms in creation, if it is *parama* – supreme, pure, high, intense, authentic – it is *bhakti*.

In Swami Niranjanananda Saraswati's (2013) words:

> The word *bhakti* comes from the root *bhaj sevayam*. By adding sufix *ktin* to the root *bhaj*, the word *bhakti* is created. *Bhakti* is a connection of love. . . .
>
> The definition of *bhakti* is an expression in life in which you experience love within yourself and through which others feel happy. *Sevā* (selfless service to others) and *prema* (unconditional love) are the only two kinds of interactions in life that have been accepted as expressions of *bhakti*.
>
> – *Bhakti Sādhanā*

3

अमृतस्वरूपा च ॥

amṛtasvarūpā ca ॥

And it, in essence, is like ambrosia.

Interpretation: Experience of *bhakti* is compared with the experience of having nectar. This word *amṛta* (ambrosia) has been used in metaphorical as well as literal sense here. Metaphorically ambrosia refers to blissfulness that arises in a *bhakta* due to his/her immersion in deep love.

Besides, when the *bhakti* becomes extremely intense and one pointed, the psychic centres begin to open in the *bhakta*'s body. In the process, when the *viśuddhi cakra* in the throat centre opens, then the *bhakta* experiences a constant flow of nectar-like sweetness in his/her throat. This is the *amṛta* that is described in the Śāstras as the liquid that drops from *bindu cakra* at the top back of the head to the *viśuddhi cakra* in the throat area.

Metaphorically, the word *amṛta* also denotes immortality. It is stated in the scriptures that drinking of *amṛta* leads to immortality. The *deva*s became immortal when they drank the *amṛta* that came out of the churning of the ocean. Sage Nārada is suggesting that *bhakti* leads to immortality as it leads to liberation from cycles of birth and death.

Two

Effects of Bhakti

4

यल्लब्ध्वा पुमान् सिद्धो भवति,
अमृतो भवति, तृप्तो भवति ॥

yallabdhvā pumān siddho bhavati,
amṛto bhavati, tṛpto bhavati ॥

Attaining *bhakti*, a person attains perfection, achieves immortality and becomes absolutely contented.

Interpretation: Sage Nārada explains the effects of *bhakti* on the seeker. He says that when human beings experience *bhakti*, they feel completeness, they break the bonds of individuality and become fully contented in their state of being.

Here the sage is addressing three chief human ambitions on earth. They are power through perfection, immortality as freedom from cycles of birth–death/joy–sorrow and peace as freedom from a web of desires.

The first expression *siddho bhavati* relates to powers through perfection. It refers to *siddhi*s which may arise in a *bhakta* due to his/her intense focus. Many *bhakta*s and *yogī*s acquire *siddhi*s – sometimes consciously and sometimes unconsciously. *Siddhi*s may come inadvertently to a seeker. The Purāṇas and the epics are full of stories of sages and *yogī*s who acquired and displayed *siddhi*s. Many modern-day *yogī*s and saints have been known to display *siddhi*s.

Sage Patañjali in his *Yogasūtra* describes the *siddhis* which are attained by a *yogī* through spiritual practices. Some common *siddhis* are: omniscience, telepathy, ability to move through space, levitation, entering another body, mastery over natural elements, etc. Patañjali, however, warns against the *siddhis*. According to him the *siddhis* are an obstacle to the final goal of self-realization.

In this *sūtra*, the sage may have used the word *siddha* in another sense. *Siddha* also refers to a perfected being. He says that a *bhakta* becomes a *siddha*. He could be suggesting that the *bhakta* realizes his/her full potential in human life.

The second expression, *amṛto bhavati* means that the *bhakta* becomes immortal. In this context, immortality means freedom from cycles of birth and death; pain and sorrow. Human life comes with three kinds of elemental suffering: *ādhidaivika*, *ādhibhautika* and *ādhyātmika*. *Ādhidaivika* suffering is caused by natural catastrophes like famine, earthquakes, floods and fires. *Ādhibhautika* suffering is caused by illnesses and diseases that humans suffer. *Ādhyātmika* suffering is felt by individual self due to its sense of separation from the Universal Self. In Swami Niranjanananda Saraswati's words:

> The cause of *ādhibhautika* suffering is wrong lifestyle, ignorance about how to live in a right way and due to fast changing situations around us which we are not able to cope with. *Ādhidaivika* suffering is related to natural calamities, earthquakes, storms, floods, etc. *Ādhyātmika* suffering is caused by spiritual emptiness in human life.

According to Sage Nārada, *bhakti* provides a relief from all kinds of suffering and hence allows the possibility of endless bliss and joy in life.

By the third expression, *tṛpto bhavati*, Nārada suggests that the *bhakta* attains absolute contentment. *Tṛpti* (contentment) is the third trait that a *bhakta* develops as a result of *bhakti*.

The sage indicates that *bhakti* induces immense contentment by inducing freedom from all kinds of desires. In Indian spiritual tradition contentment is considered to be the greatest wealth. One who has contentment is the richest person in the world.

In other words this *sūtra* emphasizes that *bhakti* is an experience that promises immense power, freedom from suffering and contentment in human life.

5

यत्प्राप्य न किञ्चिद्वाञ्छति, न शोचति,
न द्वेष्टि, न रमते, नोत्साही भवति ॥

yat prāpya na kiñcid vāñchati, na śocati,
na dveṣṭi, na ramate, notsāhī bhavati ॥

Attaining *bhakti*, he desires nothing, worries about nothing, hates nothing and gets excited about nothing.

Interpretation: In continuation with the previous *sūtra*, the sage here is describing the effects of *bhakti* experience. He says that if one experiences or attains *bhakti* then one becomes free of desires, worries, hatred and excitement. In other words all the negative tendencies which are the cause of suffering in life are automatically removed by *bhakti*.

The same view is exposited in chapter VI of the *Bhagavadgītā*. Here Kṛṣṇa tells Arjuna:

यं लब्ध्वा चापरं लाभं मन्यते नाधिकं ततं ।
यस्मिन्स्थितो न दुःखेन गुरुणापि विचाल्यते ॥ २२ ॥

yaṁ labdhvā cāparaṁ lābhaṁ manyate nādhikaṁ tataḥ ।
yasminsthito na duḥkhena guruṇāpi vicālyate ॥

– VI.22

> After having a sense of God realization, the seeker does not consider any other attainment more profitable than that. Established in that attainment, s/he is not moved even by enormous sorrow.

As humans, we are caught in a web of desires. Desires pull us into various directions and when they cannot be fulfilled, they bring immense pain and sorrow. These concentric circles of desires can be broken by one-pointed *bhakti*, which then leads to removal of nervous excitement, unnecessary attraction or repulsion in life situations. Thus, the *bhakta* achieves a state of equanimity in all situations.

6

यज्ज्ञात्वा मत्तो भवति, स्तब्धो भवति, आत्मारामो भवति ॥

yatjñātvā matto bhavati, stabdho bhavati,
ātmārāmo bhavati ॥

Knowing that (*bhakti*), the *bhakta* becomes ecstatic, spellbound and joyous within.

Interpretation: The sage explains that *bhakti* induces a kind of joyous intoxication, a sense of wonder and a sense of being complete in oneself.

Attainment of *bhakti* (deep devotion), i.e. supreme love of the Divine creates blissful joy, wonder and intoxication. Now when the *ādhyātmika* suffering is completely eliminated from the consciousness of the *bhakta*, the *bhakta* feels oneness with the Cosmic Self. He/she has touched base with his/her source and the sense of alienation from the source which causes *ādhyātmika* suffering or spiritual restlessness remains no more.

Three

Characteristics of Bhakti

7

सा न कामयमाना निरोधरूपत्वात् ॥

sā na kāmayamānā nirodharūpatvāt ॥

Being of a form that blocks the desires, it (*bhakti*) harbours no lustfulness.

Interpretation: The word *kāma* means 'desire' in general but *kāma* also refers to 'lust' or 'passion'. *Bhakti,* as a form of spiritual practice, leads to end of all desires which bind human beings in a chain of joy and sorrow. It naturally leads to renunciation of desires. So *kāma* is absent in *bhakti*.

8

निरोधस्तु लोकवेदव्यापारन्यासः ॥

nirodhastu lokavedavyāpāranyāsaḥ ॥

Nirodhaḥ is dropping off of the worldly and scriptural activities.

Interpretation: In the previous *sūtra*, the sage talks about *bhakti* having a form that effects *nirodhaḥ*. In this *sūtra,* he defines the concept of *nirodhaḥ* in relation to *bhakti* experience. He says *nirodhaḥ* is renunciation of actions of worldly as well those of scriptural nature – *laukika* and Vedic.

Literally, however, the word *nirodhaḥ* comes from root *ni* which means "to block". So *nirodhaḥ* means "to block out".

Swami Satyananda Saraswati in his description of the second *sūtra* of Patañjali's *Yogasūtra*, *yogaścittavṛtti nirodhaḥ* (योगश्चित्तवृति निरोधः), brings out this meaning of *nirodhaḥ*.

Yet, according to Nārada, in this *sūtra* we may consider that *bhakti* leads to a state of mind in which the *bhakta* is able to rise above the bondage of prescribed actions. Two kinds of *karmas* (actions) are mentioned here – *laukika* and Vedic (worldly and scriptural). All human beings have to perform action in order to exist in the body as well as in the world. In Hindu belief system these actions should be performed according to the directions given in the scriptures (here, the Vedas) and according to one's social situation. *Bhakti* allows one to renounce these rules for action. It gives freedom from scriptural as well as social bondage.

In spite of the above statement, the concept of renunciation of action has to be understood in the right spirit. Kṛṣṇa explains to Arjuna in the *Bhagavadgītā* that "no one can renounce action". One "can only renounce the fruit of the action". Here also the emphasis is on the renunciation of "the fruit" of the action and not on renunciation of "the action itself". There is difference between doing the action with a desire and doing it for the sake of maintaining the social and moral order in the family, the community and the society. The first type of action brings more bondage but the second type frees one from the bondage.

9

तस्मिन्ननन्यता तद्विरोधिषूदासीनता च।।

tasminnananyatā tadvirodhiṣūdāsīnatā ca ।।

An exclusive emotional involvement in That (God) and detachment from everything which is against That (God).

Interpretation: The sage adds one more element to his previous definition of *nirodhaḥ*. He says that *nirodhaḥ* is also *ananyatā* (something that exists in exclusion of all else). In other words one-pointed engagement with God along with detachment from everything else which may block the way to Him. *Bhakti* leads to what is called as *pratyāhāra* which means withdrawal of senses from the sense objects. In the system of *aṣṭāṅga-yoga* of Patañjali, it is the fifth limb in the sequence of – *yama, niyama, āsana, prāṇāyāma, pratyāhāra, dhāraṇā, dhyāna, samādhi – aṣṭāṅga-yoga*.

10

अन्याश्रयाणां त्यागोऽनन्यता ।।

anyāśrayāṇāṁ tyāgo 'nanyatā ।।

Giving up all other protections except that of God is *ananyatā*.

Interpretation: The sage describes meaning of *ananyatā* in the context of *bhakti* in this *sūtra*. When a devotee develops supreme faith in his/her chosen God. He/she depends only on God for everything and forgets or renounces all other dependencies. This state is called as the state of *ananyatā*. *Ananyatā* literally means "state of having no other". This is *ananyā bhakti*.

11

लोकेवेदेषु तदनुकूलाचरणं तद्विरोधिषूदासीनता ।।

lokevedeṣu tadanukūlācaraṇaṁ tadvirodhiṣūdāsīnatā ।।

To do all actions, worldly as well as scriptural, in accordance with God's will

and to have indifference, *udāsīnatā* to everything which is in conflict with that.

Interpretation: This *sūtra* describes what a *bhakta* does in *bhakti* and/or what happens to him. The sage says that a *bhakta* performs all actions, be they worldly or scriptural, in accordance with God's will. He/she becomes indifferent, *udāsīna* to everything that is not in harmony with God's will. This state of being in harmony with God's will and being in a state of indifference to everything else is understood as *udāsīnatā* with respect to worldly actions.

It is clear that Sage Nārada defines each important word and concept that he uses in his exposition of *bhakti*. For instance, in the last three *sūtras*, the connotations for the concepts of *nirodhaḥ*, *ananyatā* and *udāsīnatā* have been given.

If seen closely, these three – *nirodhaḥ*, *ananyatā* and *udāsīnatā* – could be very helpful lessons for attaining *pratyāhāra* – withdrawal of senses from external sense objects. because only when the *pratyāhāra* has taken place, can the *bhakta* direct his/her awareness to the chosen deity.

12

भवतु निश्चयदाढ्र्यादूर्ध्वं शास्त्ररक्षणम् ॥

bhavatu niścayadārḍhyādūrdhvaṁ
śāstrarakṣaṇam ॥

After one gets firmly resolved in the high state, (one) must be a firm protector of the scriptures.

Interpretation: In this and the following *sūtras*, the sage illustrates how a *bhakta* should act in the world even after getting firmly established in *bhakti*. He/she should continue with the necessary acts of life in righteous manner according to his/her station in life and in community. This way the *bhakta* protects the truth of the Śāstras (the sacred texts) which are there to maintain balance in the creation.

This *sūtra* appears to contradict with *sūtra*s 7 and 8 where the sage says that *bhakti* is *na kāmayamānā nirodharūpatvāt* and *nirodhastu lokavedavyāpāranyāsaḥ*.

If *bhakti* is renunciation of all actions related to routine life as well as those related to maintain the moral order given in the scriptures, then why does he prescribe "adherence to scriptural actions" in this *sūtra*. Perhaps, he wishes to qualify the previous *sūtra*s by suggesting that even if the seeker gets established in *bhakti*, He/she should perform actions according to scriptures in order to protect the scriptures. At social level, *bhakta*'s actions are watched closely by people around him/her, the ordinary people look up to him/her even after he/she has attained supreme *bhakti*. Thus the *bhakta*'s freedom from social or scriptural rules is only at personal level and not at the social level.

An example of why the famous or powerful people have a special duty to protect the *dharma* as given in the scriptures (*śāstra rakṣaṇam*) is given in chap. 2 of the *Bhagavadgītā* where Kṛṣṇa elaborately preaches Arjuna to perform his duty as a kṣatriya according to the Śāstras. Otherwise, he would face condemnation:

> अथ चेत्त्वमिमं धर्म्यं सङ्ग्रामं न करिष्यसि ।
> ततः स्वधार्मं कीर्तिं च हित्वा पापमवाप्स्यसि ॥
>
> *atha cettvamimaṁ dharmyaṁ saṅgrāmaṁ na kariṣyasi* ।
> *tataḥ svadharmaṁ kīrtiṁ ca hitvā pāpamavāpsyasi* ॥
>
> – *Bhagavadgītā* II.33

> If, however, you refuse to fight this righteous war, abandoning your social duty and reputation, you will certainly incur sin. – Swami Muktananda (tr.)

13

अन्यथा पातित्याशङ्कया ॥

anyathā pātityāśaṅkayā ॥

Otherwise there is danger of falling (from higher state to lower state).

Interpretation: If the *bhakta* does not protect the Śāstras and does not keep his/her actions in harmony with the Śāstras, there is a danger of falling from the higher state that he/she has attained. Hence *bhakta* must be constantly on the alert lest he/she should fall into the traps of selfish desires arising from the ego. In other words, sage is prescribing a way of acting in the world even if the *bhakta* has attained a high state. He emphasizes that the guidance of the Śāstras should be adhered to while performing actions in the world.

14

लोकोऽपि तावदेव; भोजनादिव्यापारस्त्वाशरीरधारणावधि॥

loko 'pi tāvadeva; bhojanādivyāpārastvāśarīradhā raṇā-vadhi ॥

The world exists only so long (for the *bhakta* until *bhakti* is attained). However, the body-related actions like eating and sleeping should be executed until the body is alive.

Interpretation: Nārada now talks about how the *loka*, the *saṁsāra* (the world) exists for *bhakta* only until the highest state is attained. Later the world as a space and time where ordinary individuals are bound by routine and rules of living, does not exist for the *bhakta*. This idea is in conformity with the previous *sūtra*s (5 and 6), where he talks about how the *bhakta* is not bound any more by the scriptural and worldly actions.

There is emphasis on the need to perform appropriate action also. The *bhakta* must not confuse 'liberation' with the renouncement of all action. The action is necessary as long as one is embodied. Lord Kṛṣṇa also makes it very clear in the *Bhagavadgītā* that it is only the 'fruit' of the action that is to be renounced and not the action itself. Kṛṣṇa says that the action is necessary to sustain the bodily existence. Even if one wants to renounce action, one cannot do so as long as one is embodied. Action is an inherent part of the physio-psychic structure of human beings. Living is doing. As long as we are in the body, we have to breathe, eat, sleep, eliminate, reproduce and so on and so forth.

Therefore, here it is said that even if one has attained supreme *bhakti*, one should properly perform all the actions that are due in the society as well as in the body.

Four

Opinions of Spiritual Masters (Ācāryas)

15

तल्लक्षणानि वाच्यन्ते नानामतभेदात् ।।

tallakṣaṇāni vācyante nānāmatabhedāt ।।

We will speak about features of (*bhakti*) according to diverse views.

Interpretation: The sage moves on to describe views of other scholars on *bhakti* and its characteristics. This *sūtra* reveals how a subject of enquiry was dealt in a scholarly exposition in ancient times. As Sage Nārada undertakes this work on *bhakti*, he also makes an effort to not only understand but also record and acknowledge works of other scholar-sages in the field. Later, he moves deeper into the subject and talks about it in greater detail from his own perspective. Hence follow the views of other scholar-sages on *bhakti*.

As *bhakti* is intense love for God, ways of *bhakti* are the ways of expressing that love. Different sages have talked about different ways of creating an intense relationships with the chosen form of God.

16

पूजादिष्वनुराग इति पाराशर्यः ।।

pūjādiṣvanurāga iti pārāśaryaḥ ।।

According to Sage Parāśara's son, *bhakti* is love for worship of God and other related acts.

Interpretation: Son of Parāśara is Sage Vyāsa. According to Vyāsa worship involves deep merger of senses and mind into God consciousness, therefore he prescribes worship as an important feature of *bhakti*.

Worship can be described as a kind of activity which involves showing love and reverence for a particular form of God and adoring Him with everything that is desirable to human sensibilities. Concept of *pūjā* (worship) has been described in the Śāstras (scriptures) elaborately. Most common form of worship followed in Hindu temples is the sixteen-step worship (*ṣoḍaśopacāra-pūjā*). A *bhakta* conceives God in human form, forges a relationships with Him and offers the best objects to Him. The most popular forms of God are the *avatāra*s as human beings. It is easy to make a relationship with someone conceived in one's own likeness. However, worship as such is a very gross act of offering one's favourite sense objects to one's chosen God.

The act of worship is viewed differently in Tantras. In Tantras the processes of finding oneness with cosmic reality range from gross to subtle, from ritualistic to mental appropriation.

In the *Vijñānabhairava Tantra*, the Goddess puts up a very logical question to Bhairava, the Supreme God. She asks if the whole creation is pervaded by Supreme Consciousness then who worships and to whom is the worship offered. The Bhairava gives an answer which shows the irrelevance of external worship:

Worship does not mean offering flowers.
It means offering your heart to the vast mystery of the universe

It means to let your heart pulse with the life of the universe, without thought and without reservation. It means being so in love that you are willing to dissolve and be recreated in every moment. – Roche 2014: 350

17

कथादिष्विति गर्गः ॥

kathādiṣviti gargaḥ ॥

For Garga, listening or telling the stories from God's life (is *bhakti*).

Interpretation: Sage Garga believes that listening and telling the stories and legends of God is the best form of remembrance and tribute to a beloved God. *Kathā* is recitation/narration/singing of episodes or whole life story of God. *Kathā* is a living tradition in India. *Kathākāra*s tell the stories from God's life and legends on earth and emphasize upon the lessons that mortals can draw from various episodes. Vālmīki's *Rāmāyaṇa*, Tulsīdās' *Rāmacaritamānasa* and the *Bhāgavata Purāṇa* are the most popular source texts for *kathākāra*s (the storytellers).

18

आत्मरत्यविरोधेनेति शाण्डिल्यः ॥

ātmaratyavirodheneti śāṇḍilyaḥ ॥

Rejoicing in the Supreme Self through harmony (with the self) is (*bhakti*) for Śāṇḍilya.

Interpretation: This *sūtra* talks about *ātmarati* (immersion in the joy of the self), as a characteristic of *bhakti*. The word *ātmarati* is composed of two words – *ātmā* and *rati*. *Ātmā* (the individual self) is part of *paramātmā* (the Divine Self). The word *rati* comes from the root *rat*, i.e. 'to get absolutely absorbed in something'. Hence according to Sage Śāṇḍilya, *bhakti* is to remain completely absorbed in *ātmā* which is a part of Supreme Self (*paramātmā*). Sage Śāṇḍilya believes that love of everything which is not an obstacle in being harmonious with divine self is *bhakti*.

Śāṇḍilya, interestingly is not talking about a god which is outside of us but about the divine principle which is present in each of us. So, the best form of *bhakti* according to Śāṇḍilya is that where the *bhakta* can recognize the divine within and does not see any dualism between the self and the Divine. This thought falls in line with Advaita Vedānta[1] school of Indian philosophy.

19

नारदस्तु तदर्पिताखिलाचारता तद्विस्मरणे
परमव्याकुलतेति (च) ।।

nāradastu tadarpitākhilācāratā tadvismaraṇe
paramavyākulateti (*ca*) ।।

For Nārada, however, *bhakti* is offering all actions to Him and becoming exceedingly restless on slightest forgetfulness of Him.

Interpretation: After expressing other sages' views about *bhakti*, Sage Nārada now gives his own opinion on *bhakti* in this *sūtra*. According to him surrendering all actions and

---

[1] Advaita Vedānta is a non-dualistic school of Indian philosophy exposited and systematized by eighth-century saint scholar Ādi Śaṅkarācārya. According to this system, *Brahman* is the only reality, and *ātman* (the individual soul) and the *Brahman* (the Cosmic Principle) are one.

deeds to the chosen god (the *iṣṭa devatā*) and not forgetting Him ever, is a mark of supreme love (*bhakti*). The *bhakta* becomes restless and uneasy if he/she forgets his/her God even for a moment. Nārada is suggesting that *bhakti* is the surrender of the 'doership' from our limited, egotistical self. The *bhakta* performs of all actions in constant remembrance of a higher Cosmic Principle.

In the context of remembrance, Nārada is clearly referring to the love of a chosen form of God. One prevalent view is that it is easy to love God in a form which can be conceived by human imagination. The Purāṇas, which tell the stories of God's descent on earth in human form, assume supreme importance for a *bhakta*. Through these stories, the *bhakta* gets a chance to figure out or imagine the form of God with attributes.

Here a very relevant point is raised by Y. Subrahmanya Sarma, one of the early twentieth-century English translators of this text. He notes that the *sūtras* 16 to 19 indicate a successive progression in *bhakti*. *Sūtra* 16, for instance, talks about expressing *bhakti* by doing something or by acting externally (*pūjā*); *sūtra* 17 is about expressing *bhakti* through speech; *sūtra* 18 is about expressing *bhakti* by inner means including mind; and *sūtra* 19 takes up *bhakti* in its subtlest possible expression which is complete surrender to the Divine. Hence it is suggested that body, mind, speech and action – all should be given to the Divine in order to reach the highest state of *bhakti* (Sarma 1938: 6).

20

अस्त्येवमेवम् ॥

astyevamevam ॥

It is exactly like this, like this.

Interpretation: Nārada puts double emphasis on his own definition of *bhakti* over others in this *sūtra*. According to him, a *bhakta* offers all actions to God, remembers Him in every breath and cannot bear separation from Him (remembrance of Him) even for a moment.

21

यथा व्रजगोपिकानाम् ॥

yathā vrajagopikānām ॥

Like that of the *vrajagopikās*.

Interpretation: Sage Nārada here gives an example of supreme *bhakti*, that of *vrajagopikās'* for Kṛṣṇa. *Vrajagopikās* (or *brajagopikās*) are conceived as a reincarnation of sages and saints who, as *jñāna-yogīs*, followed the path of *jñāna-yoga* (knowledge). Their path included meditation with virtues of *viveka* and *vairāgya* to attain God realization. In their previous birth, they expressed their desire to live in close proximity with God in their next lives so that they could see Him and feel Him and love Him. As a boon from God, in their next life they were born as the *vrajagopikās*. The *vrajagopikās* were the cowherdesses of Vṛndāvan where Kṛṣṇa, the *avatāra* of God Viṣṇu, came to live in human form. They loved Kṛṣṇa more than anything else in their life. The *Bhāgavata Purāṇa* reveals that the *gopikās* could not bear separation from Kṛṣṇa even for the space of time it takes to blink the eyes. These *gopikās* are depicted as married and householding women in a cowherd community but at the same time so immersed in love of Kṛṣṇa that whenever they heard Kṛṣṇa's flute, they would leave all the house work behind and would run to the bank of Yamunā, where they could see Kṛṣṇa playing His flute. They surrendered their actions to Kṛṣṇa and in their simplicity knew nothing but love for Kṛṣṇa. Once when a *jñāna-yogī* seeker, Uddhava came to these *vrajagopikās* and asked how they perform *bhakti* of *Īśvara*, they said:

> *uddho mana na bhae dasa bīsa*
> *eka huto so gayo syāma saṅga*
> *ko ārādhe īsa.*
> — *Uddhava–Gopī Saṁvāda*, Sūrdāsa
>
> Uddhava! We don't have ten or twenty hearts; there is only one which has gone with our Śyāma, now with which heart can we worship God?

22

तत्रापि न माहात्म्य-ज्ञानविस्मृत्यपवादः ॥

tatrāpi na māhātmya-jñānavismṛtyapavādaḥ ॥

In that (*gopikās* love for Kṛṣṇa) also there is no exception to their remembrance of knowledge of greatness of the Divine.

Interpretation: Sage Nārada says that in this example of *gopikās*' love for Kṛṣṇa, the *gopikās* are fully aware of Kṛṣṇa's divinity, his glory and his greatness as Supreme God. Their love arises out of their awareness of Kṛṣṇa's divinity. Their love is not a physical attraction for a handsome, flute-player or charmer; it is love for the Supreme Divine in Him.

Swami Satyananda relates this episode from the *Bhāgavata Purāṇa*, where Uddhava asks *vrajagopikās* why are they so shockingly unaware of their physical state of being. The *gopikās* replied:

> Look here, we have no mind for such things. We have only one awareness and that is of Kṛṣṇa, whom we loved and played within our youth. Physically he may not be with us, but all the time we have been thinking only about him. Sometimes this introversion and intense thought

> awareness continues all-day long and all-night long, all-week long and all-month long. So, it is impossible for us to think about our clothes and our body, or even about what others think about us.

This is the description of the state of a supreme *bhakta*. *Gopikās*' love for Kṛṣṇa is not the ordinary love of a woman for a man. It is absolute self-surrender where the awareness has become completely focused on the chosen one.

According to Swami Satyananda:

> As one treads the path of Bhakti-yoga, self-interest automatically starts to fade. There is transformation into giving and more giving. This devotion grows more and more as the awareness of the *bhakta* increases, as he recognizes and progressively removes his limitations and imperfections. The feeling of the Bhakti is intensified. The level of awareness is correspondingly intensified. The higher the level of Bhakti, the less the ego. Eventually, there is a point where there is total identification with the object of worship. – Swami Satyananda Saraswati 1992

23

तद्विहीनं जाराणामिव ॥

tadvihīnaṁ jārāṇāmiva ॥

Without this knowledge, it is just like the passionate love of a paramour for another man.

Interpretation: The sage explains the difference between love as we conceive it in human terms and the love for the Supreme which is *bhakti*. It is clear that *gopikās* were householding women and their love for Kṛṣṇa would be considered illegitimate in social terms. But since the *gopikās* had the *māhātmya-jñāna* (the knowledge of divinity) and loved Kṛṣṇa with this knowledge, their love becomes exemplary. It is the awareness that makes the difference. Without this awareness about Kṛṣṇa, their love would be nothing but another example of carnal passion of a paramour for her lover.

24

नास्त्येव तस्मिन् तत्सुखसुखित्वम् ॥

nāstyeva tasmin tatsukhasukhitvam ॥

In that kind of Love (of a paramour for a lover) happiness of the other is not happiness for the paramour.

Interpretation: Underlying message in this *sūtra* is that the love relation in which other's happiness becomes one's own is higher than the love where self-gratification is the goal. Here the sage suggests that love which is born out of sensual attraction or passion and is clandestine cannot harbour happiness. Such a love is based on duality of attraction and repulsion. If there is love today, there might be hatred tomorrow. Such a love (like the one between a paramour and her lover) acts on the principal of possession of the other. This is selfish and here the happiness of one is of no consequence to the other. Sometimes the growth of the one may even give rise to feeling of jealousy in the other. This phenomenon is common in man–woman relations which are often based on selfish possession of the other. However, a love relation, which is completely devoid of ego and is based on selfless surrender and devotion, becomes *bhakti*. This was so in the case of *gopikās*' love for Kṛṣṇa. Here the *gopikās* were aware of Kṛṣṇa's divinity and in that awareness they devoted themselves to Him.

25

सा तु कर्म-ज्ञान-योगेभ्योऽप्यधिकतरा ॥

sā tu karmajñānayogebhyo 'pyadhikatarā ॥

That is certainly superior to *karma-yoga* and *jñāna-yoga*.

Interpretation: Nārada's *Bhaktisūtras* were definitely compiled later than the *Bhagavadgītā* and the *Bhāgavata Purāṇa*. The reference to *gopikās* is a clear indication of this. Besides the whole concept of *bhakti*, as expounded in the *sūtras*, bears close resemblance to the concept of *bhakti* expounded in the *Bhagavadgītā*. Lord Kṛṣṇa has said in the *Gītā* that amongst the three paths to liberation, *bhakti-yoga* is superior to *karma-yoga* and *jñāna-yoga*. Kṛṣṇa says in the *Gītā* that action done with understanding and awareness of the divine essence within it, is *jñāna*. *Jñāna* is considered as superior to *dhyāna* (meditation on the Divine), and superior to *dhyāna* is the renunciation of fruit of all actions. This renunciation brings instant peace. Kṛṣṇa goes on to say: "the one who is selfless, compassionate, merciful, egoless; who has surrendered his/her mind and intellect to Me, such a *bhakta* is dearly loved by Me" (*Bhagavadgītā* XII.12-14).

The path of *bhakti* is considered as superior as well as easier than the other paths and methods of self-realization.

26

फलरूपत्वात् ॥

phalarūpatvāt ॥

Bhakti is of the nature of fruit itself.

Interpretation: The sage says that *bhakti* is a fruit, an end result in itself. In other words, *bhakti* does not come as a result of some difficult procedure. It is a procedure or process which is also the product, the result in itself. It is superior to *karma-yoga* and *jñāna-yoga* because in the paths of *karma-yoga* and *jñāna-yoga*, processes are involved and the seeker has to adhere to prolonged practices on their chosen path. In fact, the scriptures also mention that some time *bhakti* comes spontaneously to the followers of *karma-yoga* and *jñāna-yoga*, which also means that *bhakti* is a result of following these paths. When an individual seeker sincerely pursues his/her duties and follows his/her *dharma* without any desire for the fruit of those actions, he/she is following the path of *karma-yoga*. The path of *jñāna-yoga* is a process of deep contemplation about everything in creation. Through gradual elimination of every object and extraneous thought, the seeker arrives at the core Cosmic Principle.[2] This method is described as *nitya–anitya vicāra* (contemplation on everlasting and transitory). *Jñāna* makes a seeker's engagement with the Divine one-pointed. This single-minded contemplation of the Divine is *bhakti*. Thus the paths of *karma-yoga* and *jñāna-yoga*, if trodden well, would spontaneously lead to the experience of *bhakti-yoga*. Swami Satyananda Saraswati describes it very clearly in one of his articles on *bhakti-yoga*. To quote:

> *Bhakti-yoga* implies two things: both the path and the experience. A person can be on the path of *bhakti-yoga* and yet have no positive experience of intense *bhakti*. At the same time, a person can experience intense *bhakti* and yet not profess to be on the path of *bhakti-yoga*. Let us illustrate this more clearly by taking two examples:
>
> 1. If one is devotionally inclined, then one can follow the

[2] *Neti-neti* (not this, not this) – elimination is one of the meditative methods in the *jñāna-yoga*.

path of *bhakti-yoga*. This involves intense concentration of one's entire being on an object of devotion. This method of *bhakti-yoga* can eventually lead to a transcendental experience of overwhelming *bhakti*. Associated with *bhakti* is transcendental knowledge. *Bhakti* will become stronger and stronger with time and more experience.

2. If one is not devotionally inclined, then the other paths of *yoga* can be followed instead. These other paths will eventually lead to spiritual experience. This in turn will automatically lead to *bhakti*, for you will realize something that you did not know before. Whichever method you adopt, the result is the same. The paths of the devotional and the non-devotional individuals will eventually join.

– Swami Satyananda Saraswati 1992

27

ईश्वरस्याप्यभिमानद्वेषित्वात् दैन्यप्रियत्वात्[3] च ॥

īśvarasyāpyabhimānadveṣitvāt dainyapriyatvāt ca ॥

God also has dislike for egotistical attitude and has liking for the ones who have attitude of reliance on Him.

Interpretation: The sage says that God dislikes those who claim independence from Him due to their arrogance and egoism and He loves the *bhakta*s who have faith in Him.

In one of the previous *sūtra*s (*sūtra* 10: *anyāśrayāṇāṁ tyāgo nanyatā*) sage describes the concept of *ananyatā*. This *sūtra*

[3] The word *dainya* comes from *dīna* which literally means helpless or poor. Here the connotation is that of someone who is dependent on God.

gives a clue about *ananyatā*. God loves a *bhakta* who renounces dependence on all worldly supports and has complete faith in the support extended by God. In one of his talks, Swami Satyananda relates a very interesting anecdote from the life of Ramakrishna Paramahamsa to illustrate the concept of *ananyatā*. To quote:

> There is a story which is told about Ramakrishna Paramahamsa. One day a disciple came to him and asked, "How can I see God?" Ramakrishna said, "It is very easy. Do you love your wife, your son, your bank balance? Do you remember them often?" The man replied, "Yes, I remember them practically every moment of the day."
>
> So, Ramakrishna said, "Okay, now take that love for your wife, son and bank balance, and give it all to God. If you can love only God with that same intensity, He will come to you shortly." That man went away and started loving God. When he came back to Ramakrishna he said, "I am loving God so much that I do not remember my wife, my son and my money. However, you said that I would meet Him shortly, but it is fifteen days and I have not met Him yet."
>
> Later on, Ramakrishna was crossing the Gaṅgā in a small boat and the same disciple was accompanying him. When they reached the middle of the river, Ramakrishna tossed the man into the water and told the boatman to row on. You can just imagine the man's struggle for life. He was gasping for breath and fighting for life with every ounce of his strength.
>
> Finally, Ramakrishna went back and picked him up. When he pulled the man out of the river, he asked him, "Well, how did you feel?" The man said, "Oh it was terrible, unimaginable!" Then Ramakrishna asked, "When you were struggling for life, gasping for breath, did you ever once ask why God was not coming?" The man said, "No". Then Ramakrishna said, "Develop that".

28

तस्याः ज्ञानमेव साधनमित्येके ॥

tasyāḥ jñānameva sādhanamityeke ॥

Some say that *jñāna* (knowledge) is the means to attain that (*bhakti*).

Interpretation: Sage Nārada here gives the opinion of other masters about the relationship between *bhakti* (devotion) and *jñāna* (knowledge). He says that many scholars, teachers and masters are of the opinion that the way to *bhakti* is through *jñāna*.

29

अन्योन्याश्रयत्वमित्यन्ये ॥

anyonyāśrayatvamityanye ॥

Others say that devotion and knowledge are dependent on each other.

Interpretation: Many great masters have however related that *jñāna* and *bhakti* coexist. One cannot exist without the other. Both are interdependent. *Bhakti* leads to *jñāna* and *jñāna* leads to *bhakti*. The realized masters have always emphasized that all the spiritual paths lead to the same goal which is merger with the Divine Consciousness. A quote from Swami Satyananda's article on *bhakti-yoga*:

> All the paths of *yoga* lead to the same experience. The realization is the same; it is only the means that is different. All the paths of *yoga* aim at reducing and eventually eliminating the compulsive grip of the mind-born ego. *Bhakti* does this by identifying and relegating all of one's impulses towards an outside object of *bhakti*. Eventually

one surrenders the ego to the *guru,* the Supreme or whatever. This is not easy but it is the aim. *Jñāna-yoga* on the other hand attains the same results by intuitive realization, that the ego is not the totality of our being. This automatically reduces the hold of the ego and eventually dissolves it.

Karma-yoga attains the same end when one ceases to be the doer. *Rāja-yoga* reduces the power of the ego by exploring the mind. This leads to an understanding of the vast underlying substratum of each human being and every manifested object. This seemingly invincible ego automatically drops away when one starts to know the nature of the mind.

All the paths merge with each other, for they are like different petals on the same flower. *Jñāna* (revolutionary knowledge) leads to *bhakti* and *bhakti* leads to *jñāna*. *Karma-yoga* leads to *bhakti* and vice versa. In the beginning the aspirant must tread that path (or paths) that suits his or her temperament.

30

स्वयं फलरूपतेति ब्रह्मकुमारः ॥

svayaṁ phalarūpateti brahmakumāraḥ ॥

It is its own fruit, says Nārada.

Interpretation: Nārada, after expressing views of other masters, now expresses his own view. He says that *bhakti* is its own fruit. *Bhakti* is not necessarily a result of *jñāna, karma* or *yoga,* but it in itself is the highest achievement.

In Swami Tyagishananda's words:

> To say that *bhakti,* as spiritual realization, is its own fruit means that it has no cause or that it is not the effect of anything else. – Tyagishananda 1940: 129

Path of *bhakti* has no loopholes. In *bhakti* the path itself is also the goal. There is endless joy when the *bhakta* is remembering his/her *iṣṭa* ceaselessly. There is no scope of failure on this path. *Bhakti* is one of the finest phases in self-realization.

31

राजगृहभोजनादिषु तथैव दृष्टत्वात् ॥

rājagr̥habhojanādiṣu tathaiva dr̥ṣṭatvāt ॥

It is seen as such in the cases of king, home, food, etc.

Interpretation: Here the sage gives examples of how *bhakti* is not a means to a goal but is the goal itself. First reference is to state of being a 'king'. It is an instance of the lost child of a king. This child is brought up by a hermit in an *āśrama*. When this child becomes an adult, one day he gets to know that he is actually son of a king. In this example it is not due to his hearing the news on a particular day that the young man becomes a king's son, he was always a king's son. It is just that he did not know this earlier. Merely hearing what was hitherto unknown to him, does not make him all over again what he already was.

Second example is with reference to idea of being at 'home'. A wayfarer comes home after a long arduous journey. The wayfarer has a home and the joy of coming back to that home is so natural for him that after coming back he does not feel a sense of homelessness. Here again the 'joy' of coming back is not a result of experience of hardships or sense of homelessness during the journey.

The third example is that of idea of hunger and satiation with regard to food. When a person is hungry and eats the food and derives satisfaction from it, he/she doesn't feel hungry anymore. Now if more food is served to this person, it will not alter the state of satisfaction that he/she already has attained. Just as more food cannot add or subtract the satisfaction of one who has eaten enough, in the same way, one who has attained *bhakti* cannot add or subtract from his/her state of self-realization. Again to quote Swami Tyagishananda from his commentary to this particular *sūtra*:

> These illustrations show how spiritual practices really work. They result only in removing the obstructions to the natural experience of the Self, which is eternal and never produced by any effort on the part of man.
>
> – Tyagishananda 1940: 130

32

न तेन राजपरितोषः क्षुधाशान्तिर्वा ॥

na tena rājaparitoṣaḥ kṣudhāśāntirvā ॥

(In the above examples) not by mere knowledge of pre-existing facts will the king become a king; the hungry become satisfied; or the wayfarer find peace.

Interpretation: It has been explained in the above example that merely by the knowledge about his kingship, a king does not become a king all over again. Similarly a satiated person will not derive more satisfaction by having more food. And a wayfarer does not get more peace than he already has merely by reaching his home.

33

तस्मात् सैव ग्राह्या मुमुक्षुभिः ॥३३॥

tasmāt saiva grāhyā mumukṣubhiḥ ॥

Therefore, the seekers of salvation take to the path of *bhakti* alone.

Interpretation: *Bhakti* is the only path which is complete in itself and is easiest to follow. The paths of *jñāna* and *karma* might prove to be tricky and if not pursued with diligence and absolute awareness, they may even be misleading. But *bhakti*, supreme love for the Divine, never fails the seeker. And therefore the true seekers after *mokṣa* absorb themselves in *bhakti* alone.

Five

Means of Bhakti Propounded by the Spiritual Masters (Ācāryas)

34

तस्याः साधनानि गायन्त्याचार्याः ॥

tasyāḥ sādhanāni gāyantyācāryāḥ ॥

Sages sing[1] the means to attain that (supreme love).

Interpretation: Sage Nārada now moves on to describe the means to attain *bhakti* as sung by the masters. In *Sūtra*s 35 to 50, he exposits the approaches to *bhakti* as the well-known masters have described them. The aim of these *sūtra*s is to explain what a seeker after liberation must practise to establish the self in *bhakti*.

35

तत् तु विषयत्यागात् सङ्गत्यागात् च ॥

tat tu viṣayatyāgāt saṅgatyāgāt ca ॥

That becomes possible by renouncing objects of senses and attachment.

---

[1] The word, *gāyanti*, meaning "they sing", makes sense in the context of *bhakti* as joyous singing and dancing are associated with effulgence of love for the Divine in *bhakti* process. Most saint poets have sung in joy and their verses were later documented as *bhakti*-poetry.

Interpretation: Sage Nārada says that *bhakti* becomes possible through renunciation of sense objects and through renunciation of attachment. The word *viṣaya* (subject) here is used to refer to the objects of five senses (*jnānendriya*s). The objects that provide taste, touch, sight, smell and hearing for the sense organs of tongue, skin, eyes, nose and ears respectively are the *viṣaya*s for the senses. *Viṣaya* also means things which belong to objective reality. In common language *viṣaya* is anything that belongs to material world. The two words used in the *sūtra*, *viṣayatyāgāt* and *saṅgatyāgāt* refer to renunciation of sense-objects and the renunciation of attachment to the material world. The renunciation has to be not only at physical level but also at the mental level. Leaving sense-objects externally but remaining attached to them internally is not renunciation, it is suppression.

The word *tyāga* generally means 'renunciation'; 'abandonment'; 'relinquishment'; or 'giving up', but in the *sūtra* it means 'non-attachment'. The difference between 'non-attachment' and 'giving up' can be understood by an example. If a person likes to eat mangoes and he has to give up eating mangoes due to non-availability or physical illness and still craves for the mangoes, then it is considered as an attachment. Here the person had to give up the object due to compulsion and but still craves for it. On the other hand, if someone likes to eat mangoes and enjoys eating them but there comes a situation when he/she cannot eat mangoes anymore and doesn't crave for them, then the person is said to be not attached to the object. Hence if a person seems to enjoy the object when it is available but does not crave for the object when it is withdrawn, depicts that this person has no attachment to that object (*viṣaya*).

36

अव्यावृत्त भजनात् ॥

avyāvṛtta bhajanāt ॥

By unending, unbroken remembrance (of God).

Interpretation: The success in *bhakti* is attained by unbroken remembrance of God. Remembrance of God is emphasized in all schools of *bhakti*. But here the focus is on *avyāvṛta* (unbroken) like a circle. And the word *bhajana* comes from the root *bhaj*, which literally means 'to participate', 'to respect' and 'to absorb', 'to revere'. *Bhajana* becomes complete participation. In this context *bhajana* is that with which the *bhakta* participates in constant remembrance of God. Conventionally, *bhajana* involves singing the names and the attributes of the Divine. In the *sūtra*, the phrase, *avyāvṛtta bhajanāt*, is continuous remembrance of the Divine either through verbalized singing or through silent remembrance with every breath. Swami Paramahamsa Satyananda (1991) says:

> *Bhakti* is a path of love, and the path of love is a path of remembrance. The path of remembrance is only possible when you love someone and when you remember him or her, he or she is the only person who exists for you.

37

लोकेऽपि भगवद्गुणश्रवणकीर्तनात् ॥

loke 'pi bhagavadguṇaśravaṇakīrtanāt ॥

In the worldly existence also, by engaging in listening to and singing God's attributes (*bhakti* is attained).

Interpretation: The sage in this *sūtra* is addressing those *bhakta*s who are not *saṁnyāsin*s (renunciates). He says that *bhakti* can be realized even in the midst of everyday worldly existence. One need not renounce the world in order to become a *bhakta*. *Bhakti* can be attained while living in the world and while performing one's individual duties in one own life situation. For example, a mother, a wife, a father, a ṣon or a husband may also realize *bhakti* by listening to the attributes of the Divine or by singing *kīrtana*s eulogizing God.

38

मुख्यतस्तु महत्कृपयैव भगवत्कृपालेशाद् वा ।।

mukhyatastu mahatkṛpayaiva bhagavatkṛpāleśād vā ।।

Most of all it is attained either through blessings of a realized master or through Divine Grace, even though very little.

Interpretation: *Bhakti* (supreme love) can happen primarily through divine grace or through the blessings of great people like a *guru*, a spiritual master, a realized soul. Saints have always sung about the necessity of a spiritual master for those who wish to attain spiritual liberation.

39

महत् सङ्गस्तु दुर्लभोऽगम्योऽमोघश्च ।।

mahat saṅgastu durlabho 'gamyo 'moghaśca ।।

The company of the great is rare to find; it works in a subtle and profound manner; and is absolutely unfailing in effect.

Interpretation: The sage states in this *sūtra* that it is extremely difficult to find masters who are realized souls. Furthermore such masters teach in a manner that is not comprehensible to an unripe seeker. But if a seeker, by divine grace, is able to find a realized master then the effect of such a master's company is unique and unfailing. It is like an arrow that hits nothing but the goal. Describing the greatness of saints in the *Rāmacaritamānasa*, Goswāmī Tulsīdās says:

> सुनि समुझहिं जन मुदित मन मज्जहिं अति अनुराग ।
> लहहिं चारि फल अछत तनु साधु समाज प्रयाग ।।
> *suni samujhahiṅ jana mudita mana majjahiṅ ati anurāga* ।
> *lahahiṅ cāri phala acchata tanu sādhu-samāja prayāga* ।।
>
> – Bālakāṇḍa, *dohā* 2

> Those who listen and understand the sacred Prayāga like effect of the company of saints and who then immerse in that grace with intense love, they receive the fruits of all the four *puruṣārtha*s (*dharma*, *artha*, *kāma* and *mokṣa*) even when still living in the bodily form.

Tulsīdās says that the saints' mind always remains established in equanimity. Saints have neither friends nor enemies. They are like a fragrant flower which imparts its fragrance equally to the hand that plucks it as well as the one which keeps it. Tulsīdās also says that *binu satsaṅga bibeka nā hoī* (without *satsaṅga*, i.e. without the company of saints the sense of discrimination cannot ripen).

40

लभ्यतेऽपि तत्कृपयैव ।।

labhyate 'pi tatkṛpayaiva ।।

That (saints' company) is found only by divine grace.

Interpretation: This *sūtra* states that the company of the great and realized souls is found only through divine grace. It is said that nothing happens without the grace of God. A true seeker finds an appropriate master only if grace of God is upon him/her. However the grace of God certainly descends upon the true seeker as soon as he/she becomes ripe to receive it. Tulsīdās says:

> भक्ति सुतंत्र सकल सुख खानी। बिनु सतसंग न पावहिं प्रानी।।
> पुन्य पुंज बिनु मिलहिं न संता। सतसंगति संसृति कर अंता।।
>
> *bhakti sutantra sakala sukha khāni* ।
> *binu satasaṅga na pāvahiṁ prānī* ।।
> *punya pūñja binu milahiṁ na saṁtā* ।
> *satasaṅgati saṁsṛti kara aṁtā* ।।
>
> – Uttarakāṇḍa, *dohā* 44, *caupāī* 3
>
> *Bhakti* is freedom and is a mine of all the joys
> But one cannot find it without *satsaṅga*
> Without a cluster of good deeds, the saints do not appear
> Only saints' company ends the cycle of birth and death.

In other words, the company of saints is extremely difficult to find unless one has earned grace.

41

तस्मिंस्तज्जने भेदाभावात् ।।

tasmiṁstajjane bhedābhāvāt ।।

There is lack of duality between Him and His *bhakta*s.

Interpretation: Here in a very succinct manner, Nārada compares saints with God by saying that there is no difference between Him and his *bhakta*s. Those who attain *bhakti* become one with God and hence suffer no difference from Him. In other words He (God) and His *bhakta*s are the same. It is said that realized souls develop all the attributes of the Divine. Their grace is equivalent to divine grace. They can remove all the sorrows emerging from the three causes – *ādhidaivika*, *ādhibhautika* and *ādhyātmika*.

42

तदेव साध्यतां तदेव साध्यताम् ॥

tadeva sādhyatāṁ tadeva sādhyatām ॥

That alone should be cultivated,
that alone should be cultivated.

Interpretation: The company of the great people, the saints and the *bhakta*s who have become one with the divine, is difficult to find but that alone must be sought and cultivated by the aspirants.

Using the repetition as a tool of emphasis and using the phrase *tadaiva sādhyatāṁ* twice, Sage Nārada emphasizes upon the importance of *mahatsaṅga*, the company (*saṅga*) of the great (*mahat*) and the realized souls.

43

दुस्सङ्गः सर्वथैव त्याज्यः ॥

dussaṅgaḥ sarvathaiva tyājyaḥ ॥

Company of the evil should be avoided at
all times.

Interpretation: The seeker must make all effort to keep away from evil company. The word *dussaṅga* is composed of *duḥ* ("bad" or "evil") and *saṅga* (company). Bad company may also mean the company of those who tend to keep the seeker away from the spiritual path and 'good company' (*satsaṅga*), suggests company of those who assist the seeker further on his/her chosen path.

44

काम-क्रोध-मोहस्मृतिभ्रंश बुद्धिनाश-सर्वनाश-कारणत्वात् ।।

kāma-krodha-mohasmṛtibhraṁśa buddhināśa-sarvanāśa-kāraṇatvāt ।।

Evil company is the cause of lust, anger, obsession, memory loss, destruction of intellect and total annihilation.

Interpretation: This *sūtra* and a few more that follow bear a striking resemblance to some of the famous verses of chapter two of the *Bhagavadgītā*. Lord Kṛṣṇa tells Arjuna about this sequence of events in human mind in which *kāma* (desire) can unleash total annihilation of an individual. He describes how when the senses, along with the mind, come in contact with sense objects, there arises fascination/attachment for those objects and fascination for the sense-objects leads to desire (*kāma*) for those objects. In case of unfulfilled desire, anger (*krodha*) takes over; anger then gives rise to delusion (*sammoha*); delusion leads to loss of memory (*smṛtibhraṁśa*); loss of memory leads to loss of intelligence (*buddhivināśa*) and damaged intelligence leads to complete ruin (*sarvanāśa*) of the individual

ध्यायतो विष्यान्पुंसः सङ्गस्तेषूपजायते ।
सङ्गात्सञ्जायते कामः कामात्क्रोधोऽभिजायते ।।
कोधाद्भवति सम्मोहः सम्मोहात्स्मृतिविभ्रमः ।
स्मृतिभ्रंशाद् बुद्धिनाशो बुद्धिनाशात्प्रणश्यति ।।

dhyāyato viṣayān puṁsaḥ saṅgas teṣūpajāyate ।
saṅgātsañjāyate kāmaḥ kāmāt krodho'bhijāyate ।।
krodhād-bhavati sammohaḥ sammohāt-smṛti-vibhramaḥ ।
smṛti-bhraṁsād buddhi-nāśo buddhi-nāśāt praṇaśyati ।।

– II.62-63

In the present *sūtra*, Sage Nārada talks about the effect of evil company on the mind of the seeker. Evil company may lead the mind towards undesirable sense objects and the whole process of destruction is unleashed as it is described in the two verses of the *Bhagavadgītā* quoted above.

45

तरङ्गायिता अपीमे सङ्गात् समुद्रायन्ते ।।

taraṅgāyitā apīme saṅgāt samudrāyante ।।

Even though they (the seeds of negative attitudes mentioned above) may be just small ripples in the beginning, they become a big ocean due to contact (with evil company).

Interpretation: Nārada says that there might be tiny seeds of negative *saṁskāras* of attachment, anger, delusion, etc. in the consciousness of the seeker but with the influence of evil company, these can become immense like an ocean and may drown or destroy the seeker completely.

The metaphor of 'ocean' is often used in the scriptures for 'life in the world' with its accompanying waves of pain and joy. In the ocean of *saṁsāra*, the world, the human beings are said to be under the influence of *māyā* (illusion). Thus crossing this ocean of illusion is the main aim of the seeker and the different spiritual paths are given in the scriptures to help the seeker – *bhakti* is one of them. In the next *sūtra*, Sage Nārada alludes to *māyā* and moves on with his exposition on *bhakti*.

46

कस्तरति कस्तरति मायाम्? यः सङ्गं त्यजति, यो महानुभावं सेवते, निर्ममो भवति ।।

kastarati kastarati māyām? yaḥ saṅgaṁ tyajati,
yo mahānubhāvaṁ sevate, nirmamo bhavati ॥

Who crosses, who crosses the *māyā*?
One who renounces the company; who serves the great master and who becomes unattached.

Interpretation: A seeker who renounces the company (of evil); who keeps company with saints and serves the spiritual master; who consequently becomes detached with the external world of senses, crosses this ocean of *saṁsāra* created by *māyā*.

This *sūtra* echoes verse 20 of chap. 4 of the *Bhagavadgītā*. While Sage Nārada gives concise aphorisms, Lord Kṛṣṇa explains the theme of *tyāga* (renunciation) to Arjuna in the verse:

> त्यक्त्वा कर्मफलासङ्गं नित्यतृप्तो निराश्रयः ।
> कर्मण्यभिप्रवृत्तोऽपि नैव किञ्चित्करोति सः ॥
>
> *tyaktvā karmaphalāsaṅgaṁ nityatṛpto nirāśrayaḥ* ।
> *karmaṇyabhipravṛtto 'pi naiva kiñcitkaroti saḥ* ॥
>
> – *Bhagavadgītā* IV.20
>
> By renouncing the attachment to all actions and their consequent fruit; by becoming completely free from dependence on the world, remaining ever contented in supreme love; an individual, even though suitably performs necessary actions in life, actually always remains free.

Kṛṣṇa says that someone, who has control over body, senses, mind, intellect and ego, and has renounced all objects of desire; such a one, expecting nothing and performing the basic actions, does not accrue any sin and passes through this world in harmony.

47

यो विविक्तस्थानं सेवते, यो लोकबन्धमुन्मूलयति (यो) निस्त्रैगुण्यो भवति (यो) योगक्षेमं त्यजति ।।

yo viviktasthānaṁ sevate, yo lokabandhamunmūlayati (yo) nistraiguṇyo bhavati, (yo) yogakṣemaṁ tyajati ।।

One who applies oneself to solitude; breaks away from worldly attachments; transcends the three *guṇa*s, the three natural attributes and gives up desires of acquisition and preservation of merit.

Interpretation: Four characteristics are recounted in this *sūtra* as qualification for an aspiring *bhakta*. A *bhakta* seeks solitude, *viviktasthānaṁ* (pure and secluded place). Here is a suggestion that the *bhakta* keeps away from very crowded and very active places as these places have the potential to distract someone who is still a beginner on the path.

A *bhakta* eliminates attachment to the material world. This phrase indicates that the *bhakta* cannot be bound by behavioural patterns prevalent in the society. He/she lives by ethics and morals coming from realization of a higher truth. The rites and rituals, including the *saṁskāra*s like those of birth ceremony, sacred thread ceremony, marriage and death ceremony rituals, are not binding to a seeker.

A *bhakta* transcends the three *guṇa*s (three elemental characteristics) of nature (*prakṛti*). These are *tamas*, *rajas* and *sattva*, the tendencies of inertia, dynamism and composure respectively. The *bhakta* traverses a path which leads him/her to go beyond the three *guṇa*s – *sattva*, *rajas* and *tamas*.

All sentient beings operate under the influence of these three *guṇa*s. Dominance of *sattva* in an individual implies dominance of peace, balance, composure and contentment in his/her character. Dominance of *rajas* in an individual indicates dominance of passion, energy, activity, dynamism and presence of *vṛtti*s like *krodha* (anger), *lobha* (greed), *mada* (pride), *moha* (attachment), and *īrṣyā* (jealousy), etc. in his/her character. Dominance of *tamas* in an individual suggests dominance of traits of laziness, passivity, indolence, lethargy, inertia and basic animal instincts in that person.

Though the scriptures recommend that *sattva* is the most desirable *guṇa* and the individual soul must work towards developing *sattva*, Sage Nārada says that the *bhakta* should not remain bound even to the *sattva guṇa* and must transcend all the three *guṇa*s. In the *Bhagavadgītā* II.45, Kṛṣṇa also says to Arjuna:

> त्रैगुण्यविषया वेदा निस्त्रैगुण्यो भवार्जुन ।
> निर्द्वन्द्वो नित्यसत्त्वस्थो निर्योगक्षेम आत्मवान् ॥
>
> *traiguṇyaviṣayā vedā nistraiguṇyo bhavārjuna* ।
> *nirdvandvo nityasattvastho niryogakṣema ātmavān* ॥
>
> The Vedas have three *guṇa*s as their subject, become free of the three *guṇa*s, Oh Arjuna! Be free from duality, be established in the eternal, be rooted in the Self without concern for merit and protection of merit.

In the *Bhaktisūtra* text, the *sūtra*s from 35 to 50 describe the qualifications of a *bhakta*. These *sūtra*s bear a clear resemblance to various verses of the *Bhagavadgītā*.

It is worth noting that the *Māṇḍūkya Upaniṣad* relates four states of human consciousness, viz. *jāgrat avasthā* (waking state), *svapna avasthā* (dream state), *suṣupti avasthā* (deep-sleep state) and one which is beyond these three states of being, i.e. the *turīya avasthā*.

In the *turīya* state, the seeker transcends the three *guṇa*s. It is the *turīya avasthā* which is ideal for the *bhakta*.

The fourth characteristic of a *bhakta*, who goes beyond the illusion of *māyā*, is that he/she renounces all desire for merit or for preservation of fruits of merit.

Yogakṣemam is described as acquisition and preservation of merit or wealth. Here the phrase *yogakṣemaṁ tyajati* suggests relegation of all desire for acquisition and preservation – be it of wealth, merit, fame, bodily powers or *siddhi*s and the like. Sage Nārada lays emphasis on the absence of all kinds of desires in a *bhakta* and a seeker.

48

यः कर्मफलं त्यजति, कर्माणि संन्यस्यति,
ततो निर्द्वन्द्वो भवति ॥

yaḥ karmaphalaṁ tyajati, karmāṇi saṁnyasyati,
tato nirdvandvo bhavati ॥

He/she who gives up attachment to result of his/her actions becomes detached with all actions and thereby attains a state beyond the conflict of binaries like joy–pain, life–death, health–disease, love–hate, etc.

Interpretation: Theme of detachment from doership of the actions is further described by the sage. Here, he brings in the idea of *nirdvandvatā* (non-duality).

The seeker (*bhakta*) attains a state of non-dualism where he/she does not act on the basis of dualities like common mortals. For a *bhakta*, dualities of love–hate, friendship–enmity, joy–pain and attraction–repulsion cease to exist. He/she lives in equanimity in all situations.

49

यो वेदानपि सन्न्यस्यति, केवलमविच्छिन्नानुरागं लभते ।।

yo vedānapi sannyasyati,
kevalamavicchinnānurāgaṁ labhate ।।

One who gives up the Vedas also and finds only unbroken love for the Divine.

Interpretation: This *sūtra* appears to be paradoxical to *sūtra* 11, where Nārada recommends that the *bhakta* must execute all actions according to scriptures.

However, it is clear that this *sūtra* is coming at an advanced stage in the teaching.

It can be inferred that in the initial stages of *bhakti*, the *bhakta* must keep his/her actions in harmony with scriptures but in higher stages of *bhakti*, the seeker becomes free from the limitations prescribed in the Śāstras.

50

स तरति स तरति स लोकांस्तारयति ।।

sa tarati sa tarati sa lokāṁstārayati ।।

He crosses, he crosses (the ocean of *māyā*) and he makes other people cross.

Interpretation: In this *sūtra*, Sage Nārada completes the cycle of question and answer. He begins *sūtra* 46 with a question, "Who crosses the ocean of *saṁsāra* created by *māyā*?", then he goes on to explain in the following *sūtra*s the characteristics of a *bhakta* who can cross this ocean. Remarkably, this *bhakta*, not only crosses this metaphorical ocean of illusory existence created by *māyā* himself but also helps other people to cross it. In short, a *bhakta*, who has given up all attachment to the fruits of his/her actions and has gone beyond the conflicts like that of gain–loss, pain–sorrow and love–hate, crosses the ocean of *māyā* and helps others also.

51

अनिर्वचनीयं प्रेम-स्वरूपम् ॥

anirvacanīyaṁ prema-svarūpam ॥

The form of this love is indescribable.

Interpretation: This state of being in such a love is mystical. Nārada says that it cannot be described in words.[2]

This love for the Divine cannot be explained to the one who has not experienced it.

All the relations that operate in the world – man–woman, parent–child, friend–enemy, etc. – are fed by the ego which is a web of emotions and feelings that arise from an interaction between mind, senses and their objects. In *bhakti*, the ego is forgotten and what remains is an expansive self that can give as well as receive without any limitations of the physical and emotional self. Nārada says that this is inexplicable because it is experienced only by a few.

52

मूकास्वादनवत् ॥

[2] Sufi mystic Amir Khusrau beautifully writes about how words of a language cannot express this supreme love. In one of his compositions, he says: खुसरो बात अगम की, कहन सुनन की नाहिं । जो जाने सो कहे नहीं, जो कहे सो जाने नाहिं ॥ – *khusaro bāta agama kī, kahana sunana ki nahīṅ* । *jo jāne so kahe nahīṅ, jo kahe so jāne nāhīṅ* । (this is a discourse of intense mystery. The one who knows it, speaks not. The one who talks about it, knows it not!).

mūkāsvādanavat ||

Like the taste experienced by a speechless person.

Interpretation: The sage is comparing the state of the one who has experienced the love of Divine to the state of a dumb person who has eaten delicious food but cannot speak about it as he/she does not have access to the faculty of speech. The one who has experienced *bhakti* is like that dumb person because no human language can describe the divine experience. Human languages can only make an effort by suggesting or hinting at something closer to that experience.

53

प्रकाशते क्वापि पात्रे ॥

prakāśate kvāpi pātre ||

It reveals itself in a fit receptable somewhere.

Interpretation: *Bhakti* manifests in a person who is ripe to receive it. It can happen at any time and at any place. Hence anyone, regardless of time or space, can experience *bhakti*. It is not limited to any specific region or country or continent. *Bhakti* transcends the categories of time also (auspicious–inauspicious, day–night, etc.). It can dawn upon a seeker at any time when he/she becomes fit to receive it.

54

गुणरहितं कामनारहितं प्रतिक्षणवर्धमानं
अविच्छिन्नं सूक्ष्मतरं अनुभवरूपम् ॥

guṇarahitaṁ kāmanārahitaṁ pratikṣaṇa-

vardhamānaṁ avicchinnaṁ sūkṣmataraṁ anubhavarūpam ||

Without attributes, devoid of desires, increasing every moment, uninterrupted, exceptionally subtle and manifests in experience.

Interpretation: Nārada describes what happens on the path of *bhakti*. *Bhakti* (supreme love) is without attributes, i.e. it is beyond any linguistic expression and cannot be judged or measured by any unit of measuring. State of *bhakti* is a state of contentment, where desires of sense-gratification become silent. This is a state of ever-increasing love in which the seeker (*bhakta*) becomes open to subtler dimensions of love. There is no interruption in the flow of love in the consciousness of the lover, the *bhakta*. It is very subtle and is accessible to human experience.

Sage Nārada compared *bhakti* to supreme love in the second *sūtra*. It is unavoidable not to compare *bhakti* to "love" as human beings know it. In human experience, experience of intense "love" is closest to the *bhakti* experience. Entire tradition of *bhakti* poetry draws upon the linguistic register of love between the lover and the beloved. At the same time there is a need to qualify characteristics of human love in order to understand the experience of *bhakti* in human language. This is what the Sage Nārada is explaining through this *sūtra*.

In this *sūtra*, for instance, taking the common characteristics of human love, the sage is explaining how *bhakti* is very different from that. While human love is accompanied with attributes that go along the act of loving and being loved, for instance, beauty, youth, attraction, union, separation, time and space. The sage says that *bhakti* is beyond attributes.

Then he says that it is a state of contentment, a state where the desires are not constantly unsettling or troubling the mind. In human experience of love, there is a constant flow of desires mostly self-centred. In human love, it is common to have expectations from the beloved. The sage says, *bhakti* is *kāmanā rahitam* (devoid of desires or expectations).

Next phrase in this *sūtra* is that "*bhakti* is extremely subtle". The nature of *bhakti* is such that it is bound to be subtle. In the experience of human love, there is a tangibility and grossness because bodily form is involved, but in *bhakti* only the consciousnesses – individual and supreme – are involved. There is lack of a gross and tangible object of love in *bhakti*. The object of love is subtle and cannot be comprehended by *jñānendriyas*, i.e. the five senses which are the grossest instruments of perception. Kṛṣṇa also describes this very aptly in the *Bhagavadgītā*. He says that the mind is above the senses; the intellect is above the mind; and above the intellect is the soul. *Bhakti* is a matter of the soul (*ātmā*), which is the subtlest element of human constitution (*Bhagavadgītā* III.42-43).

Final phrase in this *sūtra* expresses that '*bhakti* is *anubhavarūpam*' which means that it is accessible to experience. In spite of it being subtlest of the subtle, it can be experienced by human beings.

55

तत् प्राप्य तदेवावलोकयति, तदेव शृणोति,
तदेव भाषयति, तदेव चिन्तयति।।

tat prāpya tadevāvalokayati, tadeva śṛṇoti, tadeva bhāṣayati, tadeva cintayati ॥

Attaining that (love), sees only that, hears only that, speaks only about that and dwells only upon that.

Interpretation: The seeker (*bhakta*), who has once partaken of this experience, cannot be attracted to anything else. He/she gets completely immersed in the experience which, being very subtle, brings intense contentment at all levels.

56

गौणी त्रिधा, गुणभेदाद् आर्तादिभेदाद् वा ॥

gauṇī tridhā, guṇabhedād ārtādibhedād vā ॥

Bhakti is of three types, if it is categorized on the basis of the *guṇa*s (*sattva*, *rajas*, *tamas*) or it may be of four types, if categorized according to types of seekers (*arthārthī*, *ārta*, *jijñāsu* and *jñānī*).

Interpretation: This *sūtra* refers to different categories of *bhakta*s. These categories are also explained in the *Bhagavadgītā* by Śrī Kṛṣṇa. *Bhakta*s can be of three types according to their predominant *guṇa*, the elemental attribute of nature. These *guṇa*s are *sattva*, *rajas* and *tamas*. Hence *bhakta*s can be sāttvic (pure with a balanced mind); rājasic (dynamic with a swaying mind); or tāmasic (indolent with a dissipated mind). Lord Kṛṣṇa describes how the *bhakta*s express their devotion in ways that are conducive to their own inner nature. For instance, a sāttvic devotee worships the effulgent beings, the *deva*s, a rājasic devotee worships the *yakṣa*s and *rākṣasa*s, and a tāmasic devotee worships the *preta*s and *bhūta-gaṇa*s (*Bhagvadgītā* XVII.4).

Besides this, in the 16th verse of chap. 7, the *bhakta*s are divided into four types according to their aspirations. In this *sūtra*, Sage Nārada refers to the first three out of these four, they are: *ārta* (distressed or the one in crisis); *jijñāsu* (those who have a deep desire to know God); *arthārthī* (those desiring wealth or other-worldly objects). Kṛṣṇa's ideal *bhakta*, however, is the *jñānī*, because the *jñānī* has one-pointed devotion towards Him and knows the essence of the Divine. Sage Nārada also gives prime place to a *bhakta* who has *ananyā bhakti*, one-pointed devotion right from the beginning of this text.

57

उत्तरस्मादुत्तरस्मात् पूर्वपूर्वा श्रेयाय भवति ॥

uttarasmāduttarasmāt pūrvapūrvā śreyāya bhavati ॥

From the succeeding ones in the sequence, each preceding one consists of higher good.

Interpretation: In this sequence of sāttvic, rājasic, tāmasic and *ārta, jijñāsu, arthārthī,* respectively, the preceding ones in each sequence are better suited for higher good than the succeeding ones. In other words the sāttvic *bhakta* is better than the rājasic and rājasic is better than the tāmasic. Similarly, the *ārta* is better than the *jijñāsu* and the *jijñāsu* is better than the *arthārthī*.

However, Sage Nārada, like Lord Kṛṣṇa, considers that the supreme *bhakta* is the one who is beyond the three *guṇa*s and three kinds of aspirations described in these categories.

58

अन्यस्मात् सौलभ्यं भक्तौ ॥

anyasmāt saulabhyaṁ bhaktau ||

Bhakti is easier to attain than other available ways (to the Divine).

Interpretation: Amongst the different forms of self-realization, *bhakti* is easy to obtain. The Śāstras, the sacred texts, emphasize that among the paths available to attain God, the path of *bhakti* is easily obtainable. In the *Bhagavadgītā*, Kṛṣṇa talks about three ways of self-realization – *karma-yoga*, *jñāna-yoga* and *bhakti-yoga*. He advises Arjuna that the path of *bhakti* is the supreme path. Tulsīdās also says in the *Rāmacaritamānasa*:

कहहु भगति पथ कवन प्रयासा।
जोग न मख जप तप उपवासा।।
सरल सुभाव न मन कुटिलाई।
जथा लाभ संतोष सदाई।।

kahahu bhagati patha kavana prayāsā |
joga na makha japa tapa upavāsā ||
sarala subhāva na mana kuṭilāī |
jathā lābha santoṣa sadāī ||
– Uttarakāṇḍa, *dohā* 45, *caupaī* 1

Tell me! What labour is there in the path of bhakti
No yoga, *no* yajña, *no* japa, *no fasting is needed*
Only simplicity; a heart without evil
And contentment with what one has got.

59

प्रमाणान्तरस्यानपेक्षत्वात् स्वयं प्रमाणत्वात् (च) ।।

pramāṇāntarasyānapekṣatvāt svayaṁ pramāṇatvāt (ca) ||

No evidence is required (to show the

supremacy of path of *bhakti*); it is evident in itself.

Interpretation: No proof is needed to ascertain whether a seeker has attained *bhakti* or not. When supreme love or devotion descends upon a seeker, it becomes self-evident in him/her. The next *sūtra* is a continuation of this one and completes the proposition stated here.

60

शान्तिरूपात् परमानन्दरूपाच्च ।।

śāntirūpāt paramānandarūpācca ।।

It reveals itself in the form of peace and supreme bliss.

Interpretation: *Bhakti* is self-evident because it manifests in the form of unending peace of mind and in the form of continual bliss and joyfulness in the *bhakta*. It is for this reason that *bhakti* is to be sought.

61

लोकहानौ चिन्ता न कार्या निवेदितात्मलोकवेदत्वात् ।।

lokahānau cintā na kāryā niveditātmalokavedatvāt ।।

(The *bhakta*) need not worry himself/herself over the miseries of the world because he/she has surrendered the self, the world and the knowledge of sacred texts to God.

Interpretation: The sage recommends that the *bhakta* should not worry about problems of the world but should do selfless service in the world to mitigate sufferings of others. When the devotee surrenders the limiting self, he/she works from a more expansive consciousness and the result is that he/she has more wisdom and more balance to handle the vagaries of life. The sage is pointing at the miseries that prevail in the world and make people suffer all kinds of sorrows. These might afflict a devotee because the devotee's heart can feel everyone's pain with same intensity as he/she would feel his/her own. The sage is also suggesting the devotee must never lose hold on his/her higher awareness in which he/she has surrendered his/her self, the whole world and the wisdom to the Supreme Power. The seeker must deal with life from this higher awareness which embraces the entire cosmos in its glance and knows its own order.

62

न तत्सिद्धौ लोकव्यवहारो हेयः किन्तु
फलत्यागहः तत्साधनं च (कार्यमेव) ।।

na tatsiddhau lokavyavahāro heyaḥ kintu
phalatyāgaḥ tatsādhanaṁ ca (kāryameva) ।।

The *bhakta* should not forsake his/her duties in the world until *siddhi* (perfection) in *bhakti* is attained. He/she should cultivate *bhakti* by surrendering the fruit of all worldly actions to the Supreme.

Interpretation: Sage Nārada is laying emphasis here on the *karma-yoga* as it is preached by Lord Kṛṣṇa in the *Bhagavadgītā*. The *bhakta* is not advised to stop performing his/her duties in the world because there is no way for him/her to remain free from action as long as he/she is an embodied creature. It is not possible not to act as long as there is a body with us. Because even to sustain the body, we have to perform actions like eating, sleeping, eliminating waste, bathing and speaking. As a result, embodied beings begin a chain of actions which are necessary just to live in the world.

> नियतं कुरु कर्म त्वं कर्म ज्यायो ह्यकर्मणः ।
> शरीरयात्रापि च ते न प्रसिद्ध्येदकर्मणः ।।
>
> *niyataṁ kuru karma tvaṁ karma jyāyo hyakarmaṇaḥ* ।
> *śarīrayātrāpi ca te na prasiddhyedakarmaṇaḥ* ।।
>
> – *Bhagavadgītā* III.8
>
> You should do the righteous actions, as performing actions is better than not performing them. Even the journey through this body cannot be accomplished without doing the actions.

In another *śloka* (V.5), Kṛṣṇa says that it is difficult for an individual to leave the idea of doership without *karma-yoga*. In other words *saṁnyāsa* is not possible without *karma-yoga*. *Karma-yoga* is integration of the idea that, "I am not the doer, I am not the doer, God only is the doer" (*nāham kartā nāham kartā, hari kartā hi kevalam*).

Kṛṣṇa says that since it is not possible and so not advisable to drop off actions, the seeker should drop off the fruit attached with the actions performed by body, mind and the senses. The seeker should surrender the fruit of the actions to God and just keep doing his/her duties in the world selflessly according to his/her situation and station in the world.

63

स्त्री-धन-नास्तिक-(वैरि)-चरित्रं न श्रवणीयम् ।।

strī-dhana-nāstika-(vairi)-caritraṁ na śravaṇīyam ।।

The seeker must not listen to the gossip

about women, wealth, atheists and enemies.

Interpretation: The seeker who is not yet ripe should not indulge in gossip about women, wealth, atheists or enemies because there is danger of distraction and thereby that of losing the path. As described in one of the *sūtra*s above, these distractions arise as small ripples initially but they may turn into a big ocean and may engulf the seeker.

64

अभिमानदम्भादिकं त्याज्यम् ।।

abhimānadambhādikaṁ tyājyam ।।

Traits like pride and vanity must be given up.

Interpretation: The seeker must shed off negative traits like pride, vanity and selfishness. Since *bhakti* has been described as "supreme love" (*parama-prema-svarūpa*), there is no place for any kind of selfishness in the practitioner of *bhakti*. When *bhakti* matures all the vices automatically drop off, but in the initial stages, the *bhakta* must make efforts to give up the negative traits in order to make fast progress on the path.

65

तदर्पिताखिलाचारः सन् कामक्रोधाभिमानादिकं
तस्मिन्नेव करणीयम् ।।

tadarpitākhilācāraḥ san
kāmakrodhābhimānādikaṁ tasminneva
karaṇīyam ।।

After offering all actions to God, the *bhakta*

should express passion, anger, pride, etc. unto Him alone.

Interpretation: One of the main qualities that a *bhakta* is expected to develop is to learn to do all actions as a medium of the divine will and to surrender the fruit of all action to the Divine. This *sūtra* advises an unripe seeker to express all emotions – negative as well as positive – towards God only. If the seeker finds traces of emotions like anger, passion, pride and attachment, lurking still in his/her consciousness, he/she can slowly get rid of them by spending them on the chosen form of God, the *īṣṭa*.

66

त्रिरूपभङ्गपूर्वकं नित्यदास्य-नित्यकान्ताभजनात्मकं
वा प्रेम (एव) कार्यं, प्रेमैव कार्यम् ॥

*trirūpabhaṅgapūrvakaṁ nityadāsya-
nityakāntābhajanātmakaṁ vā prema (eva)
kāryaṁ, premaiva kāryam* ॥

Breaking the three forms,[3] bearing a constant attitude of a devoted servant or that of a loving wife, love should be practised, love only should be practised.

Interpretation: The sage earlier mentioned that *bhakta*s can be of three kinds – sāttvic, rājasic and tāmasic or *ārta*, *jijñāsu* and *arthārthī*, respectively, depending on either the three *guṇa*s or the three aspirations. In this *sūtra*, the sage is advising that

---

[3] Here the phrase *trirūpa* with reference to Supreme Love could mean the triad of love, lover and the beloved as suggested by Y. Subrahmanya Sarma (1938) or it could mean three types of *bhakta*s mentioned above in *sūtra* 56 as *ārta*, *jijñāsu* and *arthārthī*.

the categories have to be broken or transcended. The *bhakta* must overcome the inherent *guṇa* in his/her personality and he/she must go beyond any particular aspiration and should practise love and love alone in the manner of a devoted servant or that of a loving wife.

Six

Qualities of a Supreme Bhakta

67

भक्ता एकान्तिनो मुख्याः ॥

bhaktā ekāntino mukhyāḥ ॥

The best *bhakta*s are those who have absolute dedication to God.

Interpretation: The *bhakta*s who love God for His creation and have only God and nothing else in their mind are primary amongst the devotees. Loving God with total dedication means loving God without expectations, without fear of hell or punishment. This also means loving without expectations for fulfilment of one's own desires. The phrase "Loving God with total dedication" also suggests that a *bhakta* loves God for no other reason but just because, God and the *bhakta* are a part of one expansive reality. Such *bhakta*s are in love due to exuberance of joy that arises because of full understanding and participation in God's creation.

These prime devotees generally choose a special form of God that attracts them most. They have their own chosen form or (*iṣṭa*), e.g. Śiva, Kṛṣṇa, Rāma, Jesus, Mary, Hanumān or Gaṇeśa to shower their love on. But on their journey, they become aware that God is not a person or a form but an all-pervading phenomenon, a reality that can be comprehended when they have completely given up the egotistical self. They become aware that loving God in a form is one way of experiencing that ultimate expansive reality.

68

कण्ठावरोध.रोमाञ्चाश्रुभिः परस्परं लपमानाः पावयन्ति
कुलानि पृथिवीं च ॥

kaṇṭhāvarodha-romāñcāśrubhiḥ parasparaṁ lapamānāḥ pāvayanti kulāni pṛthivīṁ ca ॥

Conversing with each other with a choked voice; with skin-hair raising with excitement, and tears flowing from their eyes, they purify their lineage as well as the earth on which they are born.

Interpretation: Taking on from the previous *sūtra*, the sage is here talking about the effect of *ekāntin bhakta*s on their surroundings. Sage Nārada calls them *ekāntin* because "they are exclusively focused in their love". These *bhakta*s leave a purifying effect on the families in which they are born and on the region in which they are born. They purify their surroundings because they have become free of all negativity and inspire positive emotions in others.

In this *sūtra*, the sage is also giving a glimpse into the behaviour of prime devotees when they meet each other. They are so overwhelmed with love that when they converse with each other tears of joy flow from their eyes and their voice gets choked due to sheer knowledge of being understood by each other. They feel intense exhilaration in the company of other *bhakta*s. Akkā Mahādevī, the twelfth-century Śaiva saint from Karnataka expresses this sentiment in one of her *vacana*s:[1]

---

[1] *Vacana* is a form of poetry that emerged in eleventh-century Karnataka when saint poets from this period sang and composed in this form. A *vacana* poem is often a non-rhyming, intense →

Associating with the ignorant
Is like to light a fire
By rubbing stones;
Associating with the wise
Is like taking butter
After churning curd.
O Chennamallikārjuna, jasmine tender,
Associating with your devotees
Is like a hill of camphor
Catching fire.

– Chaitanya 2005: 84

69

तीर्थीकुर्वन्ति तीर्थानि सुकर्मीकुर्वन्ति कर्माणि
सच्छास्त्रीकुर्वन्ति शास्त्राणि ॥

tīrthīkurvanti tīrthāni sukarmīkurvanti karmāṇi
sacchāstrīkurvanti śāstrāṇi ॥

They make the places of pilgrimages sacred; they make human actions righteous; and they impart truth to the scriptures.

Interpretation: Nārada says that the sacred places of pilgrimage where God's presence is felt intensely become sacred because of visitations by such *bhakta*s. They do their work in such a way that all actions performed by them turn out to be righteous and good. In other words, it is the *bhakta*s of this kind who set examples of righteousness in action in this world. They are the ones who add value to the Śāstras, the sacred scriptures. They, by their righteous actions, prove

---

← dialogue with a personal god. It has a soul-stirring urgency. Akkā Mahādevī, Allamā Prabhu, Basavanna and Chennabasavanna are some of the famous saint poets who used the *vacana* form.

the scriptures to be true. In other words they impart authority of truth to the scriptures.

70

तन्मयाः ॥

tanmayāḥ ॥

They are one with That.

Interpretation: The sage explains in this *sūtra* with just one word that *bhakta*s can do all that is described in the previous *sūtra* because such *bhakta*s are "full of Him". They are full of Supreme Consciousness which is of the nature of *sat–cit–ānanda* (Truth, Consciousness and Bliss). And due to their intense absorption into this consciousness, they partake of divine attributes. Hence, they sanctify all the places they tread, all the actions they perform and all the proclamations of the scriptures.

71

मोदन्ते पितरो नृत्यन्ति देवताः सनाथा चेयं भूर्भवति ॥

modante pitaro nṛtyanti devatāḥ sanāthā ceyaṁ bhūrbhavati ॥

Ancestors become happy; the effulgent beings dance in joy and this earth finds a saviour in such devotees.

Interpretation: Nārada says that such a devotee brings joy to the entire clan including the forefathers and ancestors who live unseen in different realms. Seeing such devotees, the deities rejoice because they discover someone who brings purity to all the rituals and acts of worship. And the earth feels safe, when such a devotee is born because such a devotee helps to keep the balance in the creation by keeping righteousness (*dharma*) in forefront of social order.

When an *ekāntin bhakta* takes birth, entire existence is affected by the purity of his/her consciousness which is a reflection of the Divine Consciousness. This happens because limited individual consciousness of such a *bhakta* has merged into the Cosmic Consciousness. He/she becomes an embodied representation of the Divine. The effect of this is seen in the character of the *bhakta* who becomes an image of love, grace and purity.

The sage says that seeing such a *bhakta*, whole creation experiences joy and jubilance.

72

नास्ति तेषु जातिविद्यारूपकुलधनक्रियादिभेदः ॥

nāsti teṣu jātividyārūpakuladhanakriyādibhedḥ ॥

Amongst them, no distinction can be made on the basis of caste,[2] knowledge, beauty, family lineage, wealth or profession, etc.

Interpretation: The sage comments that amongst such *bhakta*s, there is no difference due to caste, class, wealth, beauty, profession or knowledge. A *bhakta*, who has reached a level where his/her ego has completely dissolved in love of God and who is absolutely wrapped up in the love of God and is distracted by nothing, is free from all social conditioning

[2] This *sūtra* is very important as it gives us a clue about the period of composition of the text. Since Nārada is talking about irrelevance of caste in *bhakti* in this *sūtra*, it is a clear suggestion that *Nārada Bhakti sūtra* is a medieval period text when *bhakti* movement first started to question the caste system.

and its judgements. This *sūtra* shows the egalitarian attitude of the *bhakta*s.

Generally a person finds his/her individual identity and space in a society on the basis of his/her caste, family lineage, class, gender, religion, education, external beauty (here reference is to external beauty depending on skin colour, facial features, dress, make-up, etc.) and profession because the society assesses the character of a person according to these attributes. However Sage Nārada in this *sūtra* warns us to make no judgements about a *bhakta*'s devotion on the basis of such categories. A true *bhakta* is above all these distinctions.

73

यतस्तदीयाः ॥

yatastadīyāḥ ॥

Because they (the *bhakta*s) are His own.

Interpretation: Such *bhakta*s are above all categories and distinctions by which society defines the place of an individual because they are completely immersed in the expansive Divine Consciousness. They are That.

74

वादो नावलम्ब्यः ॥

vādo nāvalambyaḥ ॥

Take no recourse to argumentation.

Interpretation: The sage says that no one should enter into any controversy regarding the equality of all *bhakta*s. All *bhakta*s are of the same consciousness that has transformed into Divine Consciousness. Due to their *bhakti*, they rise above the social differences and therefore should not be judged on the basis of social distinctions. It is futile to enter into any controversy as any opposite opinion has been found untrue. *Bhakti* tradition has revealed that Divine Power has always been on the side of the *bhakta*s whenever the custodians of religion or society tried to harm them. There are examples of Mīrābāī surviving the cup of poison sent by Rāṇā's family and Kabīrdās' dead body turning into flowers when Hindus and Muslims fought claiming that Kabīr belonged to their religion.

75

बाहुल्यावकाशात्वाद् अनियतत्वाच्च ॥

bāhulyāvakāśatvād aniyatatvācca ॥

There is scope for many diverse opinions and no one opinion can be conclusive on the basis of mere reasoning.

Interpretation: In continuation with the previous *sūtra*, Nārada says that there is no need to enter into controversies because there can be many diverse opinions and yet on the basis of mere reasoning no one opinion can be authoritative. Here, Nārada is suggesting the limitations of reasoning faculty when it comes to understanding Cosmic Consciousness. Since reasoning is a faculty of the conscious mind only, it cannot take into account the rest of the mind which includes unconscious and subconscious mind. When it comes to understand the phenomena of *bhakti* or the range of consciousness of a *bhakta*, this faculty proves to be limited.

Seven

Guidelines for Bhaktas

76

भक्तिशास्त्राणि मननीयानि तदुद्बोधककर्माणि करणीयानि ॥

bhaktiśāstrāṇi mananīyāni tadudbodhakakarmāṇi karaṇīyāni ॥

Contemplating over the *bhakti* scriptures, those deeds should be performed which help to increase *bhakti*.

Interpretation: The seeker should meditate on the wisdom of devotional texts like the *Bhāgavatam*, the *Bhagavadgītā*, the *Rāmāyaṇa*, etc. and should perform such actions which lead to firmness on the path. Sage Nārada has given clear instructions to the seeker previously in the *sūtra*s 35-49 where he talked about importance of constant remembrance of God, that of *satsaṅga* and of avoidance of *duḥsaṅga* on the path of *bhakti*.

72

सुखदु:खेच्छालाभादित्यक्ते काले प्रतीक्षमाणे क्षणार्धमपि व्यर्थं न नेयम् ॥

sukhaduḥkhecchālābhādityakte kāle pratīkṣamāṇe kṣaṇārdhamapi vyarthaṁ na neyam ॥

Forsaking joy, sorrow, desire, profit, etc. not even a single moment of time should be wasted while waiting to attain the state of *bhakti*.

Interpretation: *Sukhaduḥkhecchālābhadityakte* literally means "freed from pleasure and pain and desire and profit" and *kāle pratīkṣamāṇe* means "waiting for the time".

The sage suggests that when the *bhakta* is freed from swings of happiness and sorrow, desire and profit, then he/she is left with more time than others, so he/she should use every moment of this available time in *bhakti*. In other words, once the *bhakta* becomes free from the dualistic aspects of *māyā* and he/she is able to use every spare moment of time in devotional acts as the ones described below in *sūtra* 82.

78

अहिंसा-सत्य-शौच-दयास्तिक्यादि-चारित्र्याणि
परिपालनीयानि ॥

ahiṁsā-satya-śauca-dayāstikyādi-cāritryāṇi paripālanīyāni ॥

Character traits like non-violence, truth, cleanliness (purity), mercy and faith should be preserved and maintained.

Interpretation: The seeker must adopt refined traits like truth, non-violence, internal and external cleanliness and forgiveness and should maintain them in his/her character and personality. In fact, when a *bhakta* has attained *bhakti* then purification of his/her consciousness automatically takes place and virtues appear voluntarily in the personality. However, perhaps the sage is also suggesting that in the beginning, the seeker should make some deliberate effort to stick to purer qualities of character and should not give into negative qualities like anger, greed and violence.

79

सर्वदा सर्वभावेन निश्चिन्तितैः भगवानेव भजनीयः ।।

sarvadā sarvabhāvena niścintitaiḥ
bhagavāneva bhajanīyaḥ ।।

Always and everywhere keeping oneself worry-free, the *bhakta* should worship God alone with all emotions.

Interpretation: The *bhakta* should always worship God with all his emotions – positive or negative – and he/she should leave all the worries behind.

Sage Nārada has already suggested in *sūtra* 65 (*tadarpitākhilācāraḥ san kāmakrodhābhimānādikaṁ tasminneva karṇīyam*) that the *bhakta* must direct all of his/her actions and emotions to God and should express emotions unto Him alone. Here the sage has added one aspect and that is freedom from anxiety. He says that freeing him/herself from all the worries and anxieties, the *bhakta* should worship God all the time, in all the situations of his/her life.

80

स कीर्त्यमानः शीघ्रमेवाविर्भवत्यनुभावयति (च) भक्तान् ।।

sa kīrtyamānaḥ śīghramevāvirbhavatyanubhāvay
ati (ca) bhaktān ।।

Being thus glorified (by the devotion of *bhakta*), God quickly makes Himself manifest and makes them experience self-realization.

Interpretation: When God is worshipped in such a manner (all the time, in all the situations and without worries) then He quickly appears before the *bhakta*s and makes them realize His glory. The idea presented here is that God extends His grace and gives an experience of His divinity to an *ekāntin bhakta* who has no other desire but only love for God for love's sake.

81

त्रिसत्यस्य भक्तिरेव गरीयसी भक्तिरेव गरीयसी ॥

trisatyasya bhaktireva garīyasī, bhaktireva garīyasī ॥

Of the three truths, *bhakti* only is the most powerful; *bhakti* only is the most powerful.

Interpretation: In this *sūtra*, it is not clear which three eternal truths the sage is referring to. He may be referring to the three paths of *karma-yoga*, *jñāna-yoga* and *bhakti-yoga*; he may be referring to three eternal truths – birth, life and death; he may be referring to the three divisions of time – past, present and future or he may be alluding to the three aspects of the Divine – *sat*, *cit* and *ānanda* (truth, consciousness and bliss). Within these three dimensions of the eternal, absolute Truth, the sage considers the state of *bhakti* or supreme love to be the most powerful state of being.

Some of the commentators like Swami Sivananda and Swami Tyagishananda consider the meaning of the word, *trisatyasya* as "Love of the absolute, eternal Truth" instead of taking the common meaning of the word which would be "of the three truths". So the *sūtra* is translated by the above translators as "only love of the absolute, eternal Truth is the greatest; this love indeed is the greatest".

Eight

Elevenfold Bhakti

82

गुणमाहात्म्यासक्ति-रूपासक्ति-पूजासक्ति-स्मरणासक्ति-
दास्यासक्ति-सख्यासक्ति-वात्सल्यासक्ति-कान्तासक्ति-अ
ात्म- निवेदनासक्ति-तन्मयतासक्ति-परमविरहासक्ति-रूपा
एकधा अपि एकादशधा भवति ।।

guṇamāhātmyāsakti-rūpāsakti-pūjāsakti-
smaraṇāsakti-dāsyāsakti-sakhyāsakti-
vātsalyāsakti-kāntāsakti-ātmanivedanāsakti-
tanmayatāsakti-paramavirahāsakti-rūpā
ekadhā api ekādaśadhā bhavati ।।

Although *bhakti* has one form, it can be expressed in eleven ways. These ways are: love of glorifying God's divine qualities, love of His supreme beauty, love of worship, love of remembrance, love of service to Him, love of friendship of Him, love of Him as a mother/father, love of Him as a wife, love of self-surrender to Him, love of being completely absorbed in Him, and love of Him as a beloved in separation.

Interpretation: Love for God can be expressed in any possible form. One may adopt the attitude of a beloved wife, of a friend, of a servant, of a mother or father and think of the chosen god or the (*īṣṭa*) as one's own husband, friend, master or child respectively.

This *sūtra* with its eleven forms of *bhakti* is very similar to *navadhā-bhakti* (nine forms of *bhakti*) described in the *Bhāgavata Purāṇa*. First two forms *guṇamāhātmaya* and *rūpāsakti* from this *sūtra* are subsumed under one category of *śravaṇa* in the *Bhāgavata Purāṇa*; the seventh, eighth and tenth forms , i.e. *vātsalyāsakti*, *kāntāsakti* and *tanmayāsakti* are subsumed in the *ātma-nivedana*, the ninth form given in the *Bhāgavata Purāṇa*. Today the *navadhā-bhakti* of the *Bhāgavata Purāṇa* is more popular amongst the aspirants than the *ekadaśadhā-bhakti* of Nārada. Bhakta Prahlāda, a great devotee of Viṣṇu, explains nine forms of *bhakti* as follows:

1. *Śravaṇa*: Listening to stories of adventures of God.
2. *Kīrtana*: Singing the praises of God with other *bhaktas*.
3. *Smaraṇa*: Constant remembrance of God. Fixing the attention on one's chosen god.
4. *Pāda-sevana*: Offering service at the feet of God.
5. *Arcana*: Worshipping the image of God.
6. *Vandana*: Paying homage or bowing down before God in prayer.
7. *Dāsya*: Adopting the attitude of a servant towards God.
8. *Sakhya*: Adopting attitude of a friend of God.
9. *Ātma-nivedana*: Complete self-surrender to God.

Another reference to *navadhā-bhakti* is given in Tulsīdās' *Rāmacaritamanasa*.[1] Here Lord Rāma describes nine forms of *bhakti* (3.34.4-3.35.3) which are very different from Nārada's eleven and Prahlāda's nine forms. Srī Rāma tells Śabarī about

[1] Sant Tulasīdās' *Rāmcharitamānasa*, a sixteenth century text is the latest amongst the three texts that have been quoted above. The *Bhāgavata Purāṇa* dates somewhere between 8th and 10th centuries and text of *Nārada Bhakti Sūtra* postdates the *Bhāgavata Purāṇa*.

nine steps of *bhakti*:

1. *Pratham bhagati saṁtanha kara saṅgā*: The first step in *bhakti* is *satsaṅga* (to seek the company of saints).
2. *Dūsari rati mama kathā prasaṅgā*: The second step is to be engrossed in listening to the stories about God's actions in the world.
3. *Guru pada paṅkaja sevā tīsari bhagati amāna*: Third step is selfless service to the *gurus*.
4. *Cauthi bhagati mama guna gana karai kapaṭa tajī gāna*: Fourth step is to sing praises of God without any pretentiousness.
5. *Mantra jāpa mama dṛḍha bisvāsā, pañcama bhajan so beda prakāsā*: Fifth step is to chant *mantra* of God's name with firm belief.
6. *Chaṭha dama sīla birati bahu karamā, nirat niraṁtara sajjana dharamā*: The sixth is to develop self-restraint, good conduct and detachment. Along with it, one should continuously live like a virtuous person.
7. *Sattavaṁ sam mohi maya jag dekhā, moteṅ saṁta adhika kari lekhā*: The seventh step is to develop a perception of non-duality, i.e. to see God in everything and to give high regard to saints.
8. *Āaṭhavaṁ jathā lābha saṁtoṣā, sapnehuṁ nahiṅ dekhai pardoṣā*: The eighth step is attained automatically when first seven are practised. In this state the *bhakta* sees no evil in any one and is deeply contented in his/her state.
9. *Navam saral sab sana chalahīnā, mama bharosa hīyaṁ haraṣa na dīnā*: Ninth step is also a state in which the *bhakta* has complete faith in God and becomes very simple and devoid of cunning and hypocrisy.

Although all three texts quoted above describe *bhakti* in a different vocabulary, it is clear to see that the common feature amongst all three is their focus on developing one-pointed awareness of the object of devotion.

In other words the eleven ways of the *Nārada Bhakti Sūtra* or nine ways of the *Bhāgavata Purāṇa* and those of *Rāmacaritamānasa* are meant to provide a key to engage our grosser tendencies by providing best possible nourishment to human senses. For instance, listening to, singing about, serving or being a friend, a lover and a servant to one single chosen principle are just ways of focusing physical, mental and sensual faculties of the seeker to facilitate spiritual enlightenment.

83

इत्येवं वदन्ति जनजल्पनिर्भया: एकमता:
कुमार-व्यास-शुक-शाण्डिल्य-गर्ग-विष्णु-कौडिन्य-शेषोद्धा
रुणि-बलि-हनुमद्-विभीषणादयो भक्त्याचार्या: ॥

ityevaṁ vadanti janajalpanirbhayāḥ ekamatāḥ
kumāra-vyāsa-śuka-śāṇḍilya-garga-viṣṇu-
kauṇḍinya-śeṣoddhavāruṇi-bali-hanumad-
vibhīṣaṇādayo bhaktyācāryāḥ ॥

This is the opinion of all the exponents of *bhakti* named as Kumāra, Vyāsa, Śuka, Śāṇḍilya, Garga, Viṣṇu, Kauṇḍinya, Śeṣa, Uddhava, Āruṇi, Bali, Hanumān, Vibhīṣaṇa, etc. They all unanimously express the same view without any fear of criticism from people.

Interpretation: In this *sūtra*, Sage Nārada mentions the names of all the important exponents and *ācārya*s of *bhakti* who are mentioned in the ancient scriptural texts as the great *bhakta*s. Sanatkumāra refers to Nārada's own *guru* and it is befitting that he begins with his own *guru*'s name. Vyāsa was the disciple of Nārada. Vyāsa is the author of the *Mahābhārata*. Śuka was a promulgator of *Śrīmad Bhāgavatam*. Śāṇḍilya was a contemporary of Nārada, who has also written an important text of *bhakti* called, *Śāṇḍilya Bhakti Sūtra*. Garga was an ancient sage whose teachings are recorded in the *Garga Saṁhitā*. Viṣṇu might be a reference to Rāma and Kṛṣṇa who propounded the path of *bhakti* as *avatāra*s of Viṣṇu. Kauṇḍinya was also an ancient sage and *bhakta*. Śeṣa is a reference to Ananta, who is the bearer of Mother Earth in Hindu mythology. Uddhava is mentioned as a seeker of Kṛṣṇa-Bhakti in the *Bhāgavala Purāṇa*. Āruṇi was an ancient sage famous as the knower of *Brahman*. Bali, Hanumān and Vibhīṣaṇa are the *bhakta*s whose *bhakti* for Rāma is described in detail in the *Rāmāyaṇa* and the *Rāmacaritamānasa*.

Sage Nārada here emphasizes that all the promulgators of the path of *bhakti* might differ in their emphasis but their teachings are essentially the same. The word *ādi* at the end of the list of the names indicates that the list is not conclusive. There have been and will be great *bhaktas* in the sequence of time as long as there is creation.

Nine

Phalaśruti : The Fruit of Devotion

84

य इदं नारदप्रोक्तं शिवानुशासनं विश्वसिति श्रद्धते, स भक्तिमान् भवति सः प्रेष्ठं लभते सः प्रेष्ठं लभते ॥

ya idaṁ nāradaproktaṁ śivānuśāsanaṁ viśvasiti śraddhate, sa bhaktimān bhavati saḥ preṣṭhaṁ labhate saḥ preṣṭhaṁ labhate ॥

Whoever believes and puts faith in this auspicious discipline spoken by Nārada, becomes endowed with *bhakti*. He/she finds the beloved, he/she finds the beloved.

Interpretation: In the concluding *sūtra,* the sage talks about the merits that will be attained by those who engage with this text – through reading or hearing. Two important ingredients of *bhakti* are *śraddhā* and *viśvāsa* (faith and belief). These two attributes are also the prerequisites for attaining *bhakti*. Anyone who reads or listens to the *Nārada Bhakti Sūtra* will attain the highest, says Nārada.

All sacred texts generally conclude with a verse where the author integrates his/her name along with what is called *phalaśruti,* which means description of the fruit gained by chanting or by hearing that particular text. It is keeping in line with the tradition of sacred texts that Sage Nārada not only marks his authorship by putting his name in this last *sūtra,* but that he also states the fruit which would be accrued if the text is studied with "faith and belief". Nārada makes the last *sūtra* very impressive by declaring that the fruit of studying these *bhaktisūtra*s is nothing less than an encounter with the chosen Beloved/God Himself.

॥ॐ तत् सत॥

॥ *oṁ tat sat* ॥

Glossary

Ācārya: teacher, spiritual master.

Ādhibhautika: suffering, pain or illness caused by bodily problems, wrong lifestyle, stress, etc.

Ādhidaivika: suffering caused by natural causes like floods, famines, earthquakes and storms.

Ādhyātmika: suffering emerging from spiritual vacancy.

Advaita Vedānta: philosophy of non-dualism propounded by ninth-century saint Ādi Śaṅkarācārya. According to this philosophy, *Brahman* is the only Truth. The empirical world is only an illusion created by *māyā* of *Brahman*.

Amṛta: immortal; counter for poison.

Ānanda: bliss.

Ananya: without a second; peerless.

Anubhava: experience.

Ārta: one who is afflicted; someone (who cries) in pain or suffering. Here, one crying out to God in crisis.

Arthārthī: one who has worldly desires and ambitions. Literally, "one who desires wealth".

Ātmā: individual soul, spirit.

Avatāra: descent of God on earth in human form.

Avyāvṛtta: without a break; like in a circle.

Bindu: lit. "a point". In Hindu philosophy, the whole creation arises from a *bindu* and *nāda* (*nāda-bindu*).

Bhajana: songs sung in praise of God.

Bhakta: one who has supreme love for God.

Bhakti: supreme love.

Bhakti-yoga: the path of *bhakti*.

Bhūta-gaṇas: creatures who have been in the body in the past but now live without a form. They have power to assume any form. Presumably they assume weird forms which appear to be terrible to human beings. Lord Śiva keeps them as his companions.

Brahmā: the Creator in the Trinity of Brahmā, Viṣṇu and Maheśa.

Cakra: lit. a wheel. In Tantra and Yoga philosophy, *cakra*s are psychic energy centres. There are eight important *cakra*s beginning from the root of the spine, moving upwards and culminating at the crown of the head. They are *mūlādhāra cakra, svādhiṣṭhāna cakra, maṇipūra cakra, anāhata cakra, viśuddhi cakra, ājñā cakra, bindu cakra* and *sahasrāra cakra*.

Devatā: effulgent beings who are immortal and are worshipped by human beings for various boons.

Dharma: attitude of righteousness in human beings necessary for coexistence in harmony and peace within the cosmic order. When the creation is in balance and each creature acts according to guidelines given in the scriptures, then *dharma* prevails. It is said that when evil spreads and the *dharma* deteriorates, then God comes as an *avatāra* to destroy the evil and to restore *dharma* (ref. the *Bhagavadgītā*).

Dhārmic: that which is in accordance with *dharma*.

Dhyāna: contemplation; meditation.

Ekāntin: one living in seclusion; focused on one thing.

Guṇa: an inherent quality. *Triguṇas*. *Prakṛti* manifests the world using the *triguṇa*s which are *sattva* (peace), *rajas* (dynamism) and *tamas* (passivity). The whole creation is a play of three *guṇa*s.

Guru: lit. "the one who dispels the darkness of ignorance", spiritual master, preceptor.

Īrṣyā: jealousy.

Iṣṭa: chosen form of God.

Jāgṛti: wakeful state of consciousness.

Jijñāsu: one who is eager to learn and know (about the Divine).

Jñāna: knowledge.

Jñāna-yoga: path of knowledge.

Jnānendriyas: senses of perception – nose, tongue, skin, eyes and ears.

Kāma: desire, passion.

Kāmanā: desire.

Kāmanārahitam: without desires.

Kathā: story; saga; tale; event from the life of God on earth as an *avatāra*.

Kathākāra: narrator of *kathā*.

Karma: action.

Karma-yoga: path of selfless action.

Kīrtana: act of singing God's names.

Krodha: anger.

Lobha: greed.

Loka: world.

Laukika and Vedic: worldly and scriptural.

Mada: pride.

Māhātmya: greatness of the Divine.

Māyā: the feminine energy (*śakti*) of God that creates the world of existence; considered as illusion in Vedānta philosophy.

Moha: delusion.

Mokṣa: liberation.

Neti-neti: lit. "Not this, Not this". A way of contemplation or meditation on the worldly phenomenon in which the seeker rejects all that which is transitory in order to arrive at that which is ever existing. (Literal meaning the word *Īśvara* is that which is "ever existing").

Nirdvandva: non-dual.

Nirodha: to block out.

Nitya–anitya vicāra: contemplation of that which is *nitya,* i.e. permanent and of that which is *anitya,* i.e. transitory in the existence. Path of knowledge.This is related to the concept of *neti-neti*. Both the terms are used in the context of *jñāna-yoga*.

Parama: superlative.

Paramātmā: the Supreme.

Phalaśruti: the fruit of hearing, chanting a sacred text. Traditionally all *bhakti* texts end with a *phalaśruti,* the verse in which benefits of listening or engaging with that text are listed.

Prayāga: the place of pilgrimage in Allahabad, India where sacred rivers, Gaṅgā, Yamunā and Sarasvatī meet. Also known as "Saṅgam".

Prema: love.

Preta: creatures without a human body; wandering souls who have not found peace after death.

Pūjā: worship of God.

Purāṇa: ancient texts which tell stories of gods. At least eighteen Purāṇas are popular amongst which the *Harivaṁśa Purāṇa*, the *Bhāgavata Purāṇa*, the *Śiva Purāṇa* and the *Garuḍa Purāṇa* are some of the chief Purāṇas.

Puruṣārtha: *Puruṣa* (man) + *artha* (meaning) = *puruṣārtha* (meaning of man's life). Scriptures describe the purpose of human life as *puruṣārtha*. There are four purposes that a human being strives to fulfil in life. They are *dharma*, *artha*, *kāma* and *mokṣa*. An individual primarily learns *dharma* or educates himself/herself in righteousness. Then he/she earns sufficient wealth (*artha*). Then he/she fulfils his/her desires in life (*kāma*). Finally, the individual works towards attaining liberation (*mokṣa*).

Rajas: one of the three *guṇas*. *Rajas* induces passion, energy and desires in an individual.

Rākṣasa: devil.

Rūpa: form; beauty.

Sādhanā: spiritual practice.

Sammoha: delusion.

Saṁskāra: impressions embedded in the unconscious and subconscious mind. They may be from this life and/or from previous lives.

Saṁnyāsī: one who has renounced family life or worldly transactions and is totally dedicated to self-evolution.

Sarvanāśa: annihilation of everything.

Satsaṅga: company of (or togetherness with) truth; of that which is good; of great masters; company of evolved souls.

Sattva: one of the three *guṇas*. *Sattva* induces balance, calm, creativity, peace and righteousness in an individual.

Saccidānanda: Truth, Consciousness and Bliss, the Divine Consciousness.

Śāstras: ancient sacred texts, scriptures.

Śraddhā: lit. "that which holds truth". Faith.

Ṣoḍaśopacāra-pūjā: sixteenfold worship conducted in ancient Hindu temples.

Siddhi: perfection; special divine power.

Siddha: one who has attained perfection.

Smṛtibhraṁśa: loss of memory.

Suṣupti: deep-sleep state of consciousness.

Sūtra: lit. "thread". Here, a way of expounding a chosen subject in short and terse phrases connected to each other as if by a thread (*sūtra*).

Svapna: dream state of consciousness.

Tamas: one of the three *guṇa*s. *Tamas* induces lethargy, laziness, grossness in an individual so much so that the individual cannot rise above basic instincts of *āhāra*, *nidrā*, *bhaya* and *maithuna* (food, sleep, fear and sex).

Tṛpti: contentment.

Turīya: awakened state of consciousness.

Uddhava: a character in the *Bhāgavata Purāṇa* who is a devotee of Kṛṣṇa.

Udāsīnatā: non-interest; indifference.

Vairāgya: non-attachment.

Vedic: from the Vedas, the sacred texts of knowledge.

Viveka: power of discrimination.

Viṣaya: subject; also used for 'sense' objects.

Viśvāsa: belief.

Viśuddhi cakra: the psychic centre in the spine behind the voice box.

Vivikta sthāna: a secluded and pure place.

Vrajagopikās: young cowherd women from Vṛndāvana, the mythical village where Kṛṣṇa lived in his youth.

Vṛndāvana: mythical village described in the *Bhāgavata Purāṇa*. This town still exists in Uttar Pradesh.

*Vṛtti*s: complex formations; inclinations, mental moods.

Yakṣa: beings who dwell in the city of Indra, the king of gods.

Bibliography

Chaitanya, Vinaya (tr.), 2005, *Songs for Siva: Vachanas of Akka Mahadevi*, London: Altamira Press.

Haberman, David L., 2001, *Acting as a Way of Salvation: A Study of Rāgānugā Bhakti Sādhanā*, Delhi: Motilal Banarsidass (Indian edn).

Jaggi Vasudev, Sadguru, 2017, "Accessing Higher Dimensions of Life", Youtube.Sadguru. 29.03.2017.

Kapoor, Subodh (ed.), 2002, *Sacred Sanskrit Literature* (vol. 37 of *Encyclopaedia of Indian Heritage*), Delhi: Cosmo Publications.

Kane, P.V. (ed.), 1930/1958, *History of Dharamaśāstras*, vol. 1, part 1, and vol. 5, part 2, Poona: Bhandarkar Oriental Research Institute.

Paramhamsa Satyananda, 1991, *Sayings of a Paramahansa: A Collection*, Paiania, Greece: Satayanandashram, and Munger: Yoga Publications Trust.

Roche, Lorin, 2014, *The Radiance Sutra: 112 Gateways to Yoga of Wonder and Delight*, Boulder, CO: Sounds True.

Swami Bhuteshananda, 1999, *Narada Bhakti Sutras*, Calcutta: Advaita Ashrama.

Sarma, Y. Subrahmanya (ed.), 1938, *Narada's Aphorisms on Bhakti*, Mysore: The Adhyatma Prakasha Karyalaya.

Swami Chinmayananda, 2005, *Narada Bhakti Sutra*, Mumbai: Central Chinmaya Mission Trust.

Swami Niranjanananda Saraswati, 2013, *Bhakti Sadhana*, Munger, Bihar: Yoga Publications Trust.

Swami Prabhavananda, 2000, *Narada's Way of Divine Love*, Madras: Sri Ramakrishna Math.

Swami Satyananda Saraswati, 1992, "Bhakti Yoga", *Yoga Magazine*, July.

———, 1993, *Sayings of Paramhansa*, Satyananda Ashram, Greece and Bihar School of Yoga, Munger (1st edn 1991).

Swami Satyananda Saraswati, 2004a, *Nine Principal Upanishads*, Munger, Bihar: Yoga Publications Trust (1st edn, 1975).

Swami Satyananda Saraswati, 2004b, *A Systematic Course in the Ancient Tantric Science of Yoga and Kriya*, Munger, Bihar: Yoga Publications Trust.

Swami Tyagishananda (tr.), 2001, *Nārada Bhakti Sūtras*, Chennai: Sri Ramakrishna Math.

Swami Sivananda, 1997, *Narada Bhakti Sutras*, Rishikesh: Divine Life Society.

Swami Tyagishananda, 1940, *Aphorisms on the Gospel of Divine Love or Narada Bhakti Sutras*, Madras: Sri Ramakrishna Math.

Index